RENAISSANCE
PAPERS
1967

Editor

GEORGE WALTON WILLIAMS

Assistant Editor

PETER G. PHIALAS

Published by
THE SOUTHEASTERN RENAISSANCE CONFERENCE
1968

THE SOUTHEASTERN RENAISSANCE CONFERENCE

Renaissance Papers 1967
All rights reserved
Library of Congress Catalog Card Number A 55-3551
Editorial Office
402 Allen Building, Duke University,
Durham, North Carolina 27706

Printed in Spain
for the Southeastern Renaissance Conference by
Artes Gráficas Soler, S. A.

Depósito Legal: V. 859-1968

TABLE OF CONTENTS

v

Renaissance Papers
read before the Annual Meeting
to be published or already published elsewhere.

THOMAS B. STROUP, "Religious Rite and Ceremony in Milton's Minor Poems," in *Religious Ritual in Milton's Poetry* (Univ. of Kentucky Press, 1968).

RICHARD MARIUS, "The Pseudonymous Patristic Text in Thomas More's *Confutation*," *Moreana* no. 15-16, vol. IV (Fall 1967), pp. 253-266.

The occasional illustrations are chosen from the brass rubbings on display at the University of Tennessee Center during the Conference. They are the work of Professor Isabel H. Tipton (Department of Physics, University of Tennessee), and they are reproduced here through her kindness and generosity.

Renaissance Papers

A Selection of Papers
presented at the
Twenty-fourth Annual Meeting,
April 7-8, 1967,
University of Tennessee

The papers on Milton commemorate the
tricentennial of the publication of
Paradise Lost.

Baïf's Academy and the Critics

THE *Académie de Poésie et de Musique*, founded by Jean-Antoine de Baïf and Thibaut de Courville in 1570, represents one of the first attempts in France to fuse poetry and music as a single art. It has even been suggested that this Academy was the first true Académie Française as well as the precursor of the Conservatoire. All French humanists of the sixteenth century generally understood that music and poetry were not separate arts with the Greeks ; and Baïf himself makes such a statement in a sonnet printed at the head of Costely's *Musique* in 1570, which begins :

> Jadis Musiciens et Poëtes et Sages
> Furent mesmes auteurs; mais la suite des aages,
> Par le temps qui tout change a separé les trois.

And he continues by asserting his desire to re-establish the ancient custom.

Baïf was well-acquainted with many of the leading musicians of his day, and it has even been said that he was himself a fairly proficient lutist. [1] He was, of course, perfectly aware of the popularity of music and the musical concert at court, and Jean-Baptiste-Louis Crévier rather unkindly asserts in his *Histoire de l'Université de Paris* that Baïf's motives for founding the Academy were based on pecuniary

---

[1] Eitner, Fétis and LaBorde, music historians, erroneously attribute to Baïf the words and music to an *Instruction pour toute musique des divers tons, en tablature de luth,* an *Instruction pour apprendre la tablature de guiterne,* the *Douze chansons spirituelles, paroles et musique,* and a *Un et trois livres de chansons à quatre parties,* all published in Paris during the latter part of the sixteenth century. LaBorde, in his *Essai sur la musique ancienne et moderne,* vol. II (Paris, 1780), pp. 20-21, even prints a "Chanson de Baïf" which Baïf most likely did not write.

need plus a desire to please the king, thereby gaining favorable publicity and esteem for himself.

However, according to the *lettres patentes,* issued by Charles IX in 1570, giving permission to Baïf and Courville for the establishment of their Academy, the aims of this organization were three-fold: to unite firmly music and verse; to produce a revival of the ethical effects of ancient music; and to provide for the composition, performance, and teaching of *musique mesurée.* [2] Six months later, Baïf re-affirms these aims in a letter to the king, claiming that, by the founding of this Academy, "... vostre Roiaume est le premier qui se peut affranchir de la barbarie." [3] In spite of the opposition of Parliament, Charles IX lent both financial and moral support to the Academy. This establishment was not, however, a mere series of concerts organized under royal patronage; it belonged, as Frances Yates says in her *French Academies of the Sixteenth Century,* to the "... atmosphere of Neo-Platonism in which 'music' can have more than a literal meaning, can become an 'image of the whole encyclopaedia,' covering all the disciplines, and in which the end of all artistic and intellectual effort is to purge the mind of the remnants of barbarism so that it may become capable of the highest knowledge."

As humanists, how did Baïf and his friends conceive of this music which was modeled on the ancient modes? For it was not until 1581 that Vincenzio Galilei published one of the few Greek texts which have been found on music, and sources of our knowledge of ancient music were not discovered until around 1630 and are assumed to have been unknown in the Renaissance. However, these French humanists were no doubt familiar with Plutarch's *De Musica* from the *Moralia,* an historical survey making no distinction between Greek music and poetry, Quintilian's *Institutionis Oratoriae* (lib. I, x), Plato's *Laws* (B669ff.) and Aristotle's *Poetics* (I), in which they all disapprove of the separation of poetry and music.

---

[2] See D. P. Walker's "The Aims of Baïf's *Académie de Poésie et de Musique,*" *Journal of Renaissance and Baroque Music,* I (June, 1946), 91-100. The most important sixteenth-century single source (apart from the *lettres patentes* and the statutes of the Academy), of the poetic and musical theories of Baïf's Academy is LeFevre de la Boderie's *Galliade* (Paris, 1578).

[3] This letter has been published by Léon Dorez, "Une lettre latine de J.-A. de Baïf à Charles IX," *RHLF,* II (1895), 78-81.

But it was the Italian humanists who most influenced Baïf. Marcello Ficino was a musician, a founder and a leader of the Florentine Academy who improvised music settings of Latin verses sent to him by humanist friends. This Florentine Academy, which gave real impetus to musical humanism in Italy, did not become really important until the publication in 1539 of Claudio Tolomei's *Versi e Regole de la Nuova Poesia Toscana,* an abundant collection of Italian *vers mesurés.* Tolomei founded an *Accademia della Nuova Poesia* where humanists and poets met to recite *vers mesurés,* and another group, the *Nuove Musiche,* met at the home of Count Bardi at the Tuscany Court. But the Italian humanist who most influenced Baïf's thinking in terms of the *vers mesurés* and ancient Greek music was Girolamo Mei, a friend of Tolomei, Count Bardi, and especially of Vincenzo Galilei. It was Mei, renowned for his erudition in Greek letters and music (but who, by his own admission, could neither play, sing, nor dance), who first introduced Galilei to the importance of the principle of monody. Mei's fame rests solely on a manuscript treatise concerning the Greek tonalities, *De modis musicis antiquorum* (1568), and his influence on musical development was transmitted by Galilei and Bardi among their associates of the Florentine *Camerata.* Mei, who had helped to discover Euripides' *Electra* and who was admitted to the Florentine Academy as early as 1540, came across a problem while in Rome in 1561 to which he wished henceforth to devote himself almost to the exclusion of everything else: the discovery of the nature of ancient music. Despite the difficulties of working conditions in Rome and continual ill health, he composed the *De modis musicis antiquorum* in 1568 which he completed in 1573. In this treatise, Mei seeks to reconstruct the entire body of Greek music theory within the framework of the ancient practice; therefore, Greek theory was to him the raw material of history and not a universal doctrine dictating to musicians of all times. This is precisely what differentiates Mei from other sixteenth century students of music history. Mei, the first purely historical researcher in music history, spent ten years studying only the Greek musical codices of the Vatican Library and he writes of or lists practically every theoretical source known to modern theorists of Greek music.

In 1572 Mei began a lengthy correspondence with Vincenzo Galilei, discussing at length his opinions concerning the comparative worth of

3

ancient and modern music, the use of enharmonic and chromatic genera and the ancient tunings, the styles of singing used by Olympus and Terpander, the meaning of certain obscure passages in Ptolemy, and many matters of nomenclature. [4] He particularly disagreed with Gioseffo Zarlino, who thought that counterpoint was perfection, and planned a long treatise concerning the effect of Greek music on audiences, which was never terminated due to ill health.

In 1562-1563 Baïf made a trip to Italy to attend the Council of Trent and very probably to spend some time becoming acquainted with the land of his birth. It was at that time that he met Mei, Galilei, and others associated with the Florentine Academy, and it is during this trip that he no doubt conceived the idea of his own Academy. We cannot, as so many critics have done, underestimate the importance of Mei and the Florentine Academy on the thinking of Baïf concerning Greek music and *vers mesurés*. It has also been suggested, although I do not find the argument particularly convincing, that the modes, rhythms and lost melodies of Greek poetry and music were probably found by the Academicians to exist in the medieval modes of church music. Modern musicologists concede that church music did indeed conserve these aspects of Greek music, but I think the Florentine Academy played a far more important role in influencing the *musique mesurée* of Baïf's Academy.

The regulations governing the membership and functions of this French Academy are contained in the Statutes which now form part of Vol. 13 of the *Manuscript de Conrart* at the Bibliothèque de l'Arsenal. All concerts were given at Baïf's home, the seat of the Academy, and his house has been termed the cradle of concerts in France. This house, with its exterior mottos confirming the owner's passion for ancient letters, appealed to the mind as well as to the eye. Every Sunday, members were entitled to hear a two hour performance of *vers mesurés* set to music. Three types of membership were allowed:

---

[4] See Girolamo Mei (ed. Claude V. Palisca), *Letters on Ancient and Modern Music. Girolamo Mei to Vincenzo Galilei and Giovanni Bardi* (American Institute of Musicology, n. p., 1960). The original letters are in the Regina collection of the Vatican Library and comprise the first 60 folios of a volume marked *Regina latinus,* 2021. Dragan Plamenac in 1962 published the correspondence of Mei and Bardi, a correspondence which was published as early as 1716.

the first group was made up of composers, poets and scholars; the second class of membership was restricted to the singers and instrumentalists who executed the works; and the third group consisted of listeners, both *ordinaires* and *extraordinaires*. No type of membership was voluntary; it could be obtained only by invitation or request and was subject to the approval of the entrepreneurs. No member could invite a guest to a concert without permission, and members were admitted only upon showing a special medallion which had been struck at the request of the Academy and given to each member. This medallion could not be lent or even willed to a non-member. During a performance, no one was allowed to knock, enter or leave the room, and the audience was to remain as quiet as possible. Neither could the audience go beyond the barrier of the *niche* where the musicians were playing, nor could they touch any of the books or instruments, carry away or copy any of the music. Musicians and singers, who were salaried, had to meet every day and rehearse what they had already rehearsed separately. They could not leave their duties without the consent of the masters, nor could they leave even then without first giving two months' formal notice. Any member who broke a rule was released from membership and could be re-admitted only by the consent of the entire body, after having first righted the wrong he had committed. In the case of a listener, who had to pay dues, he did not get his money back upon release from the Academy.

Not only were performances given at the Academy, but it was also established as a school, not to popularize the *musique mesurée*, but to guard it closely within a small and powerful circle until its style would become immutably fixed, its superiority recognized by the entire circle and its exponents sufficiently trained. Musicians were under the complete domination of the poets who dictated their desires and expected to have them fulfilled. However rigid the limitations of the Academy, Baïf and Courville did not lack for members. Even Charles IX attended performances enthusiastically and became their friend and benefactor.

This Academy managed to arouse the interest of the best musicians of the day, and most of them took some part in putting the *vers mesurés* to music. The two most successful composers were Claude Le-Jeune and Jacques Mauduit, although Baïf writes verse in praise of the abilities of Jean Arcadet, Pierre Cléreau, Clément Jannequin, Claude Goudimel, Courville, Guillaume Costeley, and DuCaurroy as well. Jacques Mauduit probably was the most talented composer insofar as concerns insight into the specific aims of *musique mesurée.* Claude LeJeune, a violin virtuoso, is said to have been the first to introduce that instrument into France. He was the official composer of chamber music under Henri III and Henri IV and was called "le phénix des musiciens." His *Printemps,* published posthumously in 1603, contains some of Baïf's *Chansonnettes en vers mesurés,* and his *Airs* of 1594 contain mostly verse by Baïf. Mauduit was more active in an Academy which flourished after Baïf's death, being only thirteen and therefore too young to have participated to any extent in the one of 1570; but his *Chansonnettes mesurées de Ian-Antoine de Baïf* of 1586 contain 23 measured songs of Baïf for which Mauduit wrote the music. The strife of civil war and financial difficulties cause the history of Baïf's Academy to become confused after 1571, and in 1585, it disappears altogether as an organized body. However, it reappears shortly thereafter as Guy du Faur de Pibrac's *Académie du Palais,* whose sessions took place regularly in the Louvre.

In general, Baïf's Academy was not too well accepted by his contemporaries. Therefore, in order to convince the artists' world of the value of his theories, Baïf proposed the organization of a conference to bring together all the musicians of Christendom for the purpose of testing the emotional possibilities of the music of other composers, comparing it with that produced by his Academy. This conference never did materialize, however. Those who were enthusiastic about his theories soon tired of the idea. His music was generally accepted and in vogue in 1572, but by 1576, only four years later, it was no longer pleasing, and generally the musical public returned to the favored *chanson mesurée à la lyre* and the *chanson populaire,* both of which remained popular at the court. Etienne Pasquier, in an epigram addressed to Baïf and LeJeune, praises them for their effective combining of music and verse, and he intimates that by this work they may achieve immortal fame:

> Baïf writes delicate but fiery poems
> LeJeune adds to them sweet-sounding melodies.
> One is a distinguished musician, the other a poet
> Of delicate verses, sweet tunes.

One's words nourish a honey-flowing poetry,
The other's music enlivens it.
Oh, which one of you will be Achilles,
Oh, which one of you will be Homer? [5]

Elsenwhere, he is not so kindly disposed toward Baïf's poetry when considered apart from the music. For Baïf's also attempted a spelling reform based on the one of Ramus. His *Chansonnettes* and his *Psaumes*, written for the Academy, as well as small portion of his other work, including his translation of Hesiod's *Works*, follow this spelling reform. Pasquier, in his *Recherches de la France*, claims that just one look at this written poetry discourages the reader and recalls its immediate failure: "... aussi-tost que cette sienne Poësie veit la lumiere, elle mourut comme un avorton." An anonymous poet addresses a *Xénié* to Baïf in 1572, pointing out the early favorable acceptance of the attempts of the Academy:

Whatever lacks accent and meter is not good music:
Verse which is not metrically accorded to the rules of Mathesis
Is not considered music.

In the same way that the undisciplined is considered vulgar,
That is not music which doesn't concern itself with syllable, foot and meter.
But only your rhythmic music, Baïf, can be deemed worthy of being
submitted to the judgment of Orpheus. [6]

[5]   Edit molliculos Baiffus igneis,
       Addit Iunius his melos canorŭ
       Clarus Musicus hic, & is Poeta,
       Molleis versiculi, melos suave,
       Alit mellifluam melos Poēsim,
       Viret melliflua melos Poēsi.
       Hem, quis vestrûm erit alterutri Achilles,
       Hem, quis vestrûm erit alterutri Homerus?
                 —*Epigrammaticum libri IIII* (Parisiis, 1582), p. 63.

[6]   Accĕtu numeroq; carēs bona musica non est:
       Nec breviat lōgos musica docta pedes,
       Cōsona quae versu non est numerāda Mathesis
       A doctis inter musica nulla venit.
       Quā putat ignauū, sic non est musica vulgus,
       Cui nihil sit curae syllaba, pes, numerus:
       At tua certa magis, numerosaque musica dici
       Orphî iudicio sola Baïfe potest.
                 —   *Varia epigrammata a variis auctoribus*
                       (Parisiis, 1572), fol. 4 vᵛ.

7

Four years later, in 1576, Jean LeBon, a friend of Baïf's, says of the Academy project: "However, I cannot praise Baïf enough, who has tried to correct and to place French poetry above prose, hymns, and barbarous Latin rhythms, and which, if it is not accepted by those at court, should be a certain omen and sign that learned posterity will approve his invention and correction, aside from the fact that he had too freely changed the spelling system at too early a date." Pontus de Tyard, the most learned music scholar of the Pléïade, does not deny the possibility of a non-monodic musical style, but he thinks that the verses should be rhymed. Henri Estienne approves the *vers mesurés* in his *Précellence,* but he is primarily motivated by the desire to best the Italians in some genre. DuBellay approves also, but does not write any of this verse himself. As late as 1610 we find the poet-musician Guédron composing *vers mesurés*. Gilbert Génébrard found the Academy's music neither diatonic, chromatic, nor enharmonic, but odd enough to cause the eventual failure of the Academy. D'Aubigné is not impressed with *vers mesurés* and claims that before 1540, a certain Mousset was already writing in that genre. Baillet attributes the failure of the Academy to the political and religious wars, and Goujet dislikes everything about the Academy: "Aside from the fact that *vers mesurés* are devoid of all harmony and that they are inferior to common prose, it is most disgraceful to have to spell out each word if you wish to decipher it. The entire work of Hesiod can be read in less than two hours; yet I've spent more time than that decoding fifty lines of this translation. That is a rather high price to pay for the enjoyment of this author's [Baïf's] bizarre taste."

Modern critics who are considering the value of the Academy from the point of view of poetry generally agree with Baïf's contemporaries that *vers mesurés* contributed little if anything to the advancement of French poetry. Sainte-Beuve suggests that perhaps the Academy's failure was due to the lack of a great poet to succeed Ronsard. Francis Wey, who was writing at the same time as Sainte-Beuve, is thankful that Charles IX did not live too long, for the king greatly admired Baïf and might have allowed this travesty of the French language to become established. Frémy's *Origines de l'Académie Française* in 1887 thoroughly studies Baïf's Academy from the point of view of its physical functions but does not attempt to evaluate it in an aesthetic sense.

C. H. C. Wright concludes that "Posterity has laughed at him for his pains and unjustly derided him as a pedant."

The only near-contemporary of Baïf to perceive the value of the Academy from the point of view of music history was the Père Mersenne, an early seventeenth century music critic whose opinions are valid even today. Believing passionately and emphatically in the general ethical and mimetic quality of Greek music, he highly approved Baïf's Academy for being the first in France to rediscover these truths about ancient music. It is not until the beginning of the twentieth century, however, that musicology comes into its own as discipline. In the time gap between Mersenne and the twentieth century we find only repetitions of the criticism of Baïf's contemporaries, devoid of any originality. Then in 1899, Henry Expert "rediscovers" the printed music of the Academy, presents it to his students at the Conservatoire, publishes it, and announces his intention to edit all of the *Chansonnettes* of Baïf, a task which he never completed. Marie Bobillier, writing under the pseudonym of Michel Brenet, describes the concerts given at the home of Baïf, and recognizes that these works, while not very "Greek" in nature, are exquisite, very French, and representative of a most interesting moment in the cultural history of France.

Some forty years later, musicologists revive their interest in this Academy. One possible explanation for the lack of earlier interest in Baïf's movement and indeed in French music history in general may be that until the past ten years or so, there existed no catalogue of the holdings of the Salle de la Musique of the Bibliothèque Nationale. Frances Yates' *French Academies of the Sixteenth Century,* published in 1947, is the most complete modern work on this subject. Although Yates does make two mentions of Girolamo Mei, she does not emphasize the profound influence that this Italian humanist exercised on Baïf. D. P. Walker's articles appearing in various issues of the *Musica Disciplina* from 1946-1949 thoroughly evaluate the aims of the Academy from the point of view of music history and explain in detail the Renaissance conception of *musique mesurée*. François Lesure has done much research concerning hitherto unknown facts about the lives and works of various musicians connected with Baïf's Academy, reevaluating their work in the light of modern music history. He considers this Academy a most valuable contribution to music history.

9

None of these critics, however, mention the praise and criticism that Pasquier gave to the Academy. Neither do they mention Jean LeBon's appraisal of this institution nor consider the possible importance of Pierre d'Attaignant, the first music publisher in France, who began his career under François Ier and who was a friend of Baïf's father. He and his successors, Ballard and Leroy published virtually all of the music printed in France during the sixteenth and the early seventeenth centuries. D'Attaignant was at least partly responsible for Baïf's initial interest in music and Leroy was a member of the Academy.

Although this Academy of Baïf's failed for lack of financial support, although critics contemporary with Baïf were correct in blaming the failure also on the unnecessary and cumbersome spelling reform which he tried to institute, and although most of the poetry produced by these academicians (and chiefly Baïf) was decidedly second-rate, early critics with the exception of the Père Mersenne failed completely to appreciate the value of this *Académie de Poésie et de Musique* in terms of music history. Walker, Lesure and Yates, all of the Warburg Institute, have correctly reiterated the importance of this Academy for music history. Recordings have been made by choral groups in Paris of some of the *chansonnettes* of Mauduit and of fourteen of the songs of the *Printemps* of LeJeune, which certainly serve to convince one of the beauty of the music. [7] The rhythm appears to foreshadow certain aspects of modern syncopation, and the harmonies are truly pleasing to the ear. Alas for Baïf the poet, we cannot say that the poetic aspirations of the Academy, which he deemed of utmost importance, were in any way successful except that the poetry serves as a rather pleasant accoutrement to the delightful and most interesting music executed by his composers. It is the music, not the poetry, which preserves for posterity the importance of Baïf's Academy.

Mississippi State University   BARBARA A. TERRY

---

[7] Mauduit's version of "Voicy le vert et beau May" appears on a record entitled *Chansons de la Renaissance*, recorded in Paris by the Philippe Caillard vocal ensemble for Erato Records (EFM 42021). The Jean-Paul Kreder Ensemble of Paris has recorded the *Printemps* (14 songs) of LeJeune for Le Chant du Monde. This recording is distributed in the United States by Nonesuch Records, H-100.

Politic and Moral Maxims in Tassoni's *Annali*

WHEN MILTON first set foot in Italy Alessandro Tassoni had been dead for three years, and it is doubtful, had he been living, that the young English poet would have sought him out in his retirement at his native Modena. Nevertheless, the two men had much in common: firmness of character, penetrating minds, love of liberty, love of country, and ample literary power lodged in both the left hand and the right. It is not unfitting, therefore, on this occasion when we celebrate the third centennial of the publication of *Paradise Lost*, that we should also remember Milton's older contemporary in Italian letters.

Everyone — at least everyone in this audience — remembers Tassoni, *il padre del riso,* the father of laughter, as author of that jocose epic, *La Secchia Rapita* (Paris, 1622). Most will at least have heard of his prose ten-book *Pensieri diversi* (1620). Some may also recall him as author of two fiercely patriotic *Philippics* (n. p.; *ca.* 1614/15) against the hated Spaniards, *i Signori Spagnuoli,* who had gobbled up his beloved Italy; and a few of the pedants among us, if there be any, may even remember that he was responsible (in his irresponsible youth, of course) for a pair of critical commentaries on Petrarch [1] and Dante [2] which scandalized his contemporaries by suggesting that the poetry of those two venerable bards might contain certain inanities. But I would be willing to bet my battered Borsalino that not more

---

[1] *Considerazioni sopra le Rime del Petrarca* (Modena, 1609).
[2] *Ragionamento ... intorno ad alcune cose notate nel Canto XII dell'Inferno di Dante (ca.* 1595/6). Some of Tassoni's *Postille* to the *Divine Comedy* were edited in 1821 at Reggio Emilia; later, by G. Rossi, *Studi e ricerche tassoniane* (Bologna, 1904).

than one per cent of even this distinguished group have ever thought of him as author of a whopping big set of *Ecclesiastical Annals*. I hasten to add, in your defense, that this oversight on your part need occasion neither embarrassment nor alarm. Even the specialists who have written about Tassoni have been extravagantly sparing, not to say misleading, in their references to these *Annals* — which is understandable, considering that the work has to this day remained in a manuscript [3] of which, because of its length, there can assuredly be but few copies.

The particular manuscript which I have consulted for your benefit reposes, or rather sprawls, on the shelves of my own study. It consists of four fat folio volumes, beautifully written in a painstaking *cancelleresca* hand, and extends to 1523 leaves, or something over 3000 pages. It is as long, that is to say, as fifteen to twenty typical whodunits or ten more respectable modern novels. You don't sit down and whip through it between the morning coffee-break and the taking of afternoon tea and crumpets. So far as I know, the only other copy [4] in America is that in the Folger Library's great collection of Strozziana.

Being for the moment specifically concerned with a minute segment of this vast and fascinating compilation, I can here speak in only the most general terms of its intention, value, and range of contents and interest. Those literary historians and critics who casually refer to the work as a compendium of the twelve volumes of Cardinal Baronius' *Ecclesiastical Annals* gravely mislead their readers and bear witness to their own lack of perception. It is *that;* but it is also something more and something quite different. The spirit of contradiction was strong in Tassoni, who had no high opinion of *il Baronio*. The intention of his work is, indeed, to *correct* (if not even to chastise) Baronius and to add "molt'altre cose non dette dal Cardinal Baronio e da altri Autori" (title page). He is much concerned with the theory of writing history, which he thinks Baronius did badly; what he adds is often of secular concern, mixed with much philosophical reflection and personal observation. No other of his works, in fact, tells us so much about the mind of Alessandro Tassoni.

---

[3] The autograph is preserved in the Biblioteca Estense, Modena.
[4] Slightly imperfect, lacking some leaves at the beginning.

Internal evidence indicates that the *Ristretto de gli Annali* was written *ca.* 1619-1621. Cardinal Baronio was long dead. [5] And it was just as well for Tassoni: the reading of the scornful *Ristretto* could only have made of that powerful prelate the bitterest of enemies. It was just as well, also, for other reasons, that the work was not published. Its unrelenting exposure of Papal arrogance, greed, and depravity would certainly have earned for its author a roasted carcass in the *Campo di Fiori*.

Fortunately for Tassoni, he died peacefully in his bed and with the blessing of the Church. Fortunately for us, the *Ristretto de gli Annali* and its author escaped the flames, that "Christian charity" customarily extended by the Curia in those days to its critics. And so, at last, after this long preamble, we may now turn to the examination of those moral and politic *sentenze,* or maxims, which constitute so interesting a part of Tassoni's work.

These are scattered throughout the *Annali* and number well over five hundred. A few, not more than two dozen, are in Latin and represent conventional tags. Some are obviously proverbial and are occasionally so identified in the text; and a few others are indentified by reference to a literary source. The rest are in the vulgar tongue and, while not always without antecedents and parallels, seem mostly to represent the original reflections and experiential observations of the author. In my manuscript they are commonly identified by a pair of marginal slash-marks, and they occur, generally, as a kind of epigrammatic summation of a preceding narrative. My final quotation in this paper will illustrate the typical pattern.

From this rich supply, bypassing the strictly "moral" sayings and those others, equally pungent, which relate to Church and clergy, I propose to consider a sampling of those rather numerous brief ones concerned directly with *lo Stato* and *i Principi*. Taken all together these constitute a miniature handbook for princes, a sort of mirror for magistrates. You will hear in them overtones and echoes from Machiavelli's *Prince* and *Discourses,* from the innumerable commentaries on Cornelius Tacitus, or from such encyclopedic collections as the widely circulated *Propositioni, overo Considerationi in materia*

[5] Cesare Baronio, 1538-1607.

13

di cose di Stato, a work containing the politic observations, the "leggi, regole, precetti, & sentenze" (title page) of the three Francises: Guicciardini, Lottini, and Sansovino. But besides these rumblings and reverberations you will also hear, I trust, the voice of one who had had much personal experience with Princes of both Church and State — and had, at last, no longer any faith in either.

Lesson No. One: "A Principi grandi conuiene obbedire, o ritirarsi molto lontano" (I, 11). Lesson No. Two: "I Principi mirano sempre a temperare la fortuna de' Vassali potenti" (I, 14). Lesson No. Three: "... non può uiuere appresso il Principe chi pretende al Principato" (I, 61). Lesson No. Four: "Anche a i Principi buoni dispiace la souerchia libertà di parlare" (I, 82) — "A loosely buttoned lip displeases even *good* princes." [6] Lesson No. Five: "E' temerità lo scherzare con le Tigri" (I, 86v) — "It is temerity to tickle the bellies of tigers." Lesson No. Six: "Non è mai tanto buono un Principe, che non lassi che correggere nel suo Gouerno" (I, 117v). Lesson No. Seven: "Il fauore de Principi pazzi è una imbriacatura, che spesso uccide, perciò che essi amano, et odiano a capriccio" (I, 151) — "The favor of foolish princes is a moonshineliquor drunkenness, which often kills; for they love and hate at random." Lesson No. Eight: "I Principi crudeli odiano le memorie della loro crudeltà, quantunque la stimano ... ottimo mezzo da conseruar l'Imperio" (I, 182v). Lesson No. Nine: "Della morte de Tiranni si rallegrano anche quelli istessi, che hanno riceuuti benefizi da loro" (I, 257). Lesson No. Ten (with an eye on Ch. XVIII of Machiavelli's *Prince*): "A Principi Grandi non mancano mai pretesti da rom[p]ere i patti" (I, 261v). Bonus Lesson, for good behavior: "Le carezze, che fanno i Principi sospettosi sono come le Pillole dorate, che dentro ascondono l'amaro" (I, 154). All these lessons, and many similar ones, you may learn from the first volume of the *Ristretto*.

Of course, among so many, even a few *princes* may be good fellows — you can tell them by their white hats. And this is how you may expect them to act, or these the virtues they ought to wear, remembering always that "A' Principi buoni Dio tiene le mani sopra" (I, 390):

---

[6] I preserve here and elsewhere a few of my more outrageous departures from literal translation.

... i Principi buoni non fanno mai azioni cattiue con disegno, che ne risulti loro bene (I, 12v).

Il Principe è un publico benefattore, e niun uizio lo fa più odioso dell' Auarizia (I, 77v).

I Principe prudenti amano la Religione, ma abborriscono le superstizioni, e l'Imposture (I, 144v).

I Principi non douerebbono far minor conto dell'onor di Dio, che del proprio (II, 20v).

Sotto i Principi grandi le memorie illustri si onorano, sotto i Tiranni s'abbruciano (II, 109).

I Principi di ualore tutti gli altri cercano d'amicarsegli, ma li Dappochi nessuno ne tien conto (II, 160v).

... la fama d'un Principe ualoroso può rimetter il credito perduto da cento pusillanimi (II, 169v).

L'esempio del Principe è il più efficace di tutti (II, 204v).

La Benignità stà sempre bene ne i Principi, ma non bisogna esserne prodigo con gl'Indegni (III, 18).

E' cosa da Principi prudenti il non lasciare auuicinare Esercito al suo Stato (III, 371).

I Principe saui non deuono approbare subito le nouità senza ueder prima, se sono cose utili, e di durata (IV, 14v).

Princes who follow these counsels of perfection there may be, doubtless. But where are they to be found? In Utopia, in the Land of Cockaigne. Things being as they are in this world, *i più della folla* — that is, 99.44 per cent of the total — are likely to be of another cut, their conduct less exemplary. Writers who would undertake to recount *their* lives would ordinarily have to be flatterers (III, 27), and when it comes to "writing the history of living Princes it is necessary either to be a liar or to jest with the gallows" [7] (III, 53v). Or, put another way, "l'augurar bene a Principe cattiuo, non si può fare di buona uoglia, e l'augurarli male, non si può fare senza pericolo" (I, 42). Instead of being properly disposed toward heaven, most princes "hanno sempre più cura delle Gabelle, che della Religione" (II, 322). If they pay any attention at all to religion, it is commonly to use it as *ragione di stato* (IV, 78v). For that matter, says Tassoni, "la Teologia de' Principi deue essere il sapersi conseruare il Dominio" (I, 318); and "la ragione di Stato acciesa alle uolte la ragione di Dio" (I, 341). For that matter, again, "vanno male i negozi, quando i Principi Se-

---

[7] Original: "A scriuere l'Istoria de Principi uiui, o bisogna esser bugiardo, o scherzare con le forche."

colari in cambio d'attendere al buon gouerno dello Stato si danno a correggere gli Antifornarij" (III, 76) — that is, when they fall to meddling with the Church's business. If it were otherwise, Tassoni would suspect, with Dante, [8] that wires had somehow got crossed; for it does sometimes happen that "alcuni si fanno Religiosi, che starebbono meglio Principi, et alcuni sono Principi, che starebbono meglio Monaci" (II, 301v). You just don't expect too much from these old, inveterate sinners; and, generally, these "Principi scellerati sono inesorabili ne' delitti de gli altri" (I, 88). The only thing to do with such princes is to bear with them and leave their final accounting to God: "... i Principi comunque cattiui si deuono rispettare, e lasciare il gastigo a Dio" (II, 128).

But what about the new and possibly inexperienced prince, not yet hardened in his iniquity, that famous *principe nuovo* of Machiavelli? Tassoni also has some remarks for and about him:

L'inesperienza del Principe, è la uentura del Ministro accorto (III, 256v).

... de Principi nuoui sempre ogn'uno ne spera meglio (IV, 12).

... chi mira ad assodare il Dominio con fondamenti Reali non si cura di uanità (I, 20v).

Nelle Fazioni non si deue tanto grauare una parte, che l'altra diuenga arrogante (I, 64v).

[il Principe] per tristo, e scellerato che sia ne primi anni del Gouerno procura di parer buono, per stabilirsi nello Stato (I, 92v).

A i Principi nuoui non manca altro se non la Gloria, e però quelli, che hanno spirito, premono in questo solo con ogni studio (I, 96v).

I Sudditi sono tanto fedeli quanto ueggano preualersi, o equiualersi il Principe; ma se l'abbandona la Fortuna, e lo tradisce, anch'essi l'abbandonano, e lo tradiscono (I, 97v).

Non è prudente consiglio de' Principi il metter con violenza le mani nell'antiche Religioni de Popoli (I, 113v).

I Principi Saui premono più in far osseruare le Leggi uecchie, che in farne delle nuoue (I, 144).

L'inclinazione del nuouo Principe si comincia subito a conoscere da' Ministri ch'egli elegge [9] (I, 182).

— and Tassoni, perhaps remembering his own poor luck in relatives or merely fed to the teeth with Papal nepotism, wryly observes that

---

[8] *Paradiso*, VIII, 142-148.

[9] See also I, 171v: "Dall'elezione de' Ministri si conosce l'inclinazione de Principi."

"vanno male le cose, quando i Cattiui Ministri sono Parenti del Principe" (I, 158). The outsider hasn't a chance.

Here I must arbitrarily turn the tap on this unexhausted flow of *sentenze,* even though those cited constitute but a thimbleful from the reservoir. One doesn't have to drink the whole ocean to discover its salt savor, and already I begin to see the brine encrusting your ears. Still, I should feel that you were being cheated if I did not share with you one further small squirt of isolated quickies bespeaking the wit of the author of the *Secchia*:

> I Popoli scorticati uendono alle uolte molto cara la pelle (I, 22).
> Con gli ostinati ci uuol l'Accetta (II, 18v) — "For the pigheaded, there's no remedy but the hatchet."
> I Principi, che non si contentano del suo molte uolte lasciano l'Vnghie in quel d'altri (IV, 198).
> E' spedito quel Principe, che non hà chi l'ami (I, 90) — "It's curtains for that prince who has no one to love him."

And now, good moral people, *you* would feel that you were being cheated if I did not serve up at least one of the simply "moral" sentences in the *Ristretto*. So here it is — and in context, drawn from the year of Our Lord 936, and the first year of Pope Leo VII:

[Sigonius relates] that a war having sprung up between the Greeks who were in Italy and the Prince of Benevento, the latter called in to aid him Theobald, Marquis of Spoleto and Camerino, a relative of King Hugo, who, as many Greeks as he caught, had them castrated. So that a good woman, wife to one of the Greeks made prisoner, came to plead with Theobald for her husband, and said to him that if her husband had offended, he should be punished in that which was his own and not his wife's, for it was an unjust thing that an innocent such as she should have to suffer punishment for the misdeeds of her husband; therefore let him be blinded rather than deprived of what was properly hers. Theobald, moved to laughter at her plea, was content to deliver up to her her husband intact. — "*Timely jests are dews which extinguish the blaze of wrath*" (III, 378v).

And that's the way it was in 1620, *nel tempo del buon Tassoni, il padre del riso.*

Duke University   JOHN L. LIEVSAY

W. Leonard Grant

Obiit

November 5, 1967

Two Latin Poems on Lucrezia Donati

W HEN WE turn to the vernacular Italian poems of Lorenzo de'
Medici of Florence, we discover, first, that they are of remarkably high quality indeed, and, second, that the youthful poet was (in
the words of William Roscoe) "not insensible to that tender passion
which has at all times been the soul of poetry, and has been so
philosophically and variously described in his ... writings." Lorenzo,
however, never once names his lady-love: Petrarch, in Italian and
Latin poems alike, never lets us forget the name Laura, and everyone
knows about Dante's Beatrice; but Lorenzo has studiously avoided all
mention of the name of the sovereign of his affections, although he
was by no means chary of celebrating her charms and describing their
effect upon himself, in sonnets, canzoni, and other forms of verse.

The sonnets in particular rise and fall through every degree of the
amatory thermometer: he freezes, he burns; he sings of the raptures
of sense, and then applauds a severity of virtue that no solicitation
could move; she smiles, she frowns; she refuses, she relents; she
is absent, she is present; she intrudes upon his solitude by day, or
visits him in his nightly dreams.

But this idyll was shattered by the crude realities of dynastic
arrangements: by marriage, in a word. We are told of one French
gentleman of the seventeenth century who, on being approached by his
son with the words, "Father, they tell me I'm getting married!" replied,
"Son, mind your own business!" Lorenzo's father, Piero de' Medici,
arranged a marriage between Lorenzo (now 21) and Clarice, daughter
of Giacopo Orsini, of that noble Roman family so long rivals of the
Colonnas. Like Edward Gibbon in rather different circumstances,
Lorenzo sighed as a lover but obeyed as a son — or so we may suppose. In any case, he was betrothed to Clarice Orsini in December of

1468. The earlier, unnamed sweetheart was herself briskly married off at about the same time; but we know that Lorenzo was her cavalier at his famous tournament or joust *(Giostra)* in February of 1469, where the Queen of Love and Beauty was not Clarice, but the sweetheart herself, as is clear from (for example) Luigi Pulci's *La Giostra fatta dal Lorenzo il Magnifico.*

But, as Roscoe says in discussing Lorenzo's sonnets, having thus far traced the passion of Lorenzo, may we now be allowed to ask who *was* the object of so refined a love? Indeed we may. And, fortunately, the friends of Lorenzo were not in this respect equally delicate with himself. Poliziano, in his *Stanze per la Giostra di Giuliano* (the later joust of 1475, [1] celebrated in Naldo Naldi's Latin *Hastiludium*) has praised the lady under the name of Lucrezia. Niccolò Valori tells us that Lucrezia belonged to the noble family of Donati, adding (inevitably) that she was equally distinguished for her beauty and for her virtue. Lucrezia Donati, then, was her name, and this is the lady to whom Lorenzo had paid chivalric court ever since 1464 (at which time *he* was sixteen, and she, save the mark, was only twelve); this is the lady who was affianced and wed to Niccolò Ardinghelli, but even so was still Lorenzo's lady, Queen of the joust of 1469, when Lorenzo was almost 22 and Lucrezia was nearly 17. [2]

It would not, I suppose, be impossible to think of the relationship as an actual liaison, for it is true that the fifteenth century was an age when the sins of the flesh were very much taken for granted: one Duke of Ferrara, for instance, considered a fine portrait of his illegitimate daughter no inappropriate gift to send to his own fiancée. And as for Lucrezia Donati's extreme youth, we can note that John Evelyn, the English diarist, married a girl of twelve. But for all that, in the Florence of the fifteenth or any other century, an actual liaison with so youthful an unmarried daughter of so extremely prominent, wealthy,

---

[1] At which the Queen of Love and Beauty was Simonetta Vespucci, whose features we know from the paintings of Sandro Botticelli.

[2] It is unfortunate that the portrait-bust of Lucrezia in the Victoria and Albert Museum is a forgery of the 1860's, produced by Giovanni Bastiniani, who has been called one of the two or three cleverest imitative sculptors who ever lived. It is noticeable that in this portrait-bust Lucrezia's features are almost identical with those of Ginevra de' Benci, whose portrait, painted by Leonardo da Vinci, was recently acquired by the National Gallery in Washington.

and aristocratic a family would have brought (to say the very least) discredit on the whole Medici family. [3]

In any case, once the *Giostra* of 1469 was over (in which, incidentally, Lorenzo won the first prize of a silver helmet, even though, as he remarked in his *Ricordi*, "Neither my years nor my blows were anything much!"), Lorenzo's passion for Lucrezia appears to have subsided, and the *coup de grâce*, one may be sure, was given to it when Lorenzo's wife took up Lucrezia as a friend and stood godmother to her little son.

* * *

Today I should like to examine two Latin poems on Lorenzo and Lucrezia, both of which were certainly written in 1464, two poems by men who were close friends and almost exactly precise contemporaries of each other, poems that are of different genres, to be sure, yet identical in content and intention, so much so that it would be difficult to know which influenced which: totally similar, they are nevertheless totally dissimilar. I propose to say a word or two about each poet, then read to you my English verse-translation of each poem, comment briefly on their similarities and dissimilarities, and then, to avoid going on and on about it, sit down. Polonius warns me that brevity's the *soul* of wit, but tediousness the limbs and outward flourishes.

* * *

One of the two poets in question was Naldo Naldi of Florence (1436-ca. 1513), one of the best-known and certainly one of the most prolific of the many Neo-Latin poets who enjoyed the friendship and patronage of three generations of the Medici family — Cosimo, Pater Patriae; Piero, il Gottoso; and Lorenzo, il Magnifico. In the course of his long and extremely busy life, Naldi attempted a truly remarkable variety of Latin verse-forms — lyric, invective, encomium, reflective verse, religious verse, pastoral, elegy, epigram, epillion, epic, didactic verse, and more besides. His activity as a writer extends from 1513

---

[3] But the mother (1478) of Giuliano's illegitimate son Giulio (the later Pope Clement VII) was Antonia Gorini, not a servant-girl, or a mulatto slave, as was the mother of Giulio's own son, Alessandro de' Medici (Alessandro il Moro).

to 1514, a period of over sixty years. Much of his work is ephemeral, a good deal is second-rate, some is very well worth reading, all is of historical importance. Many of the epigrams (for all of Benedetto Varchi's notorious outburst) would not have disgraced even Poliziano himself, while many of the elegies (e. g., that on the death of Cosimo de' Medici) combine forceful expression with power of feeling and imagination.

The other poet is usually called Ugolino Verino. In actual fact his name was Ugolino dei Vieri: his surname, Latinized as Verinus, became Verino, and thus he is styled today. [4] He was born at Florence in 1438, being, then, only two years younger than Naldi; he lived until 1516.

Naldi's verse-production was extensive; Verino's, though not nearly so varied as Naldi's, was positively vast, and not a great deal of it has been published: most of it is still in manuscript in the Medicean Library. One of his earliest works was the *Paradisus* (dedicated to the memory of Cosimo de' Medici), a work inspired partly by Cicero's *Somnium Scipionis*, partly by Dante's *Paradiso;* it was itself destined to be the model, in 1492, for the *Alfonsus* of Battista Spagnuoli, "good old Mantuan." Probably written in 1468, it is a curious work of versified and Platonized Christianity; Plato himself appears in the place of honour in Paradise (Aristotle is nowhere to be seen), which, however, is not astonishing, since Lorenzo's Neo-Platonic circle turned the study of Plato almost into a cult and had an eternal flame burning before a bust of the philosopher at Lorenzo's villa at Montevecchio. By 1480, Verino had completed the *Carlias,* a chivalric epic on the exploits of Charles VIII of France. By 1485, he had finished the seven books of the *Epigrammata* and had sent the dedication-copy to Mathias Corvinus of Hungary, hoping for patronage. The death, at the age of eighteen, of Ugolino's only son Michele caused the father to turn to religious poetry: in 1491, for instance, he dedicated to Savonarola his *Carmen de felicitate Christianae religionis et vitae monasticae.* In 1498 he was, as a follower of Savonarola, condemned to forfeit public office for three years. But for the next eighteen, until his death in 1516, he continued to write indefatigably.

[4] So Antonio dalla Paglia became successively Antonius Palearius and Antonio (or Aonio) Paleario.

22

His earliest work, even earlier than the *Paradisus*, I have not yet mentioned. This has been published in a critical edition by Luciano Mencaraglia [5] in 1940 — the *Flametta*, an elegiac sequence (1463-64) in two books of about fifty poems each. In Book One the poet traces the course, in separate elegiac poems, of an early love-affair with a girl he calls Flametta: the same sort of elegiac love-sequence was written by Cristoforo Landino in his *Xandra*, by the younger Strozzi in his *Silvae*, by the Flemish Johannes Secundus in his *Elegiae*, by the German Conrad Celtis in poems *(Amorum libri iv)* that might well be called *The Four Winds of Love* (he celebrates four young ladies, in the north, south, east and the west of Germany). Dozens of other Neo-Latin poets did the same in every country of Europe, except Spain. The second book of Verino's *Flametta* consists of occasional poems, complimentary addresses, poems on friends, and the like, and it is here that we find the poem on Lorenzo and Lucrezia.

* * *

So much, then, for the two poets in question. In 1464, each wrote a poem on Lucrezia Donati and Lorenzo de' Medici, and it is these two poems that I should like to present to you now. In Naldi's first eclogue [6] Daphnis is Lorenzo (*daphné* = laurus = Lorenzo, Laurentius) and the unnamed Nymph is Lucrezia (her name is hinted at, however), and here it is:

> The shepherd Daphnis once, disposed to dream,
> Adored the fairest Nymph of Arno's stream.
> Now, as he drives his flocks to verdant plains
> (The sheep and cows alike), he thus complains:
> "Too cruel far, have I deserved your scorn,   5
> That you should flee my suit, both night and morn?
> Thus doves, with trembling wing, the eagle flee,
> Thus fearful lambs the raging lion see!
> Fear not, I pray, nor spurn my loving mind:
> No harm I purpose; my intent is kind.   10

[5] In the series *Testi umanistici inediti o rari* (Florence).

[6] On Naldi's life and poems, see various essays of mine in *Manuscripta*, VI (1962), 131-154; VII (1963), 3-17, 90-102; *Studies in Philology*, LX (1963), 606-617; *Rassegna Volterrana*, XXXII (1965), 3-21.

As yet my skin is smooth, my eyes are bright:
Why flee my presence, then? Why flee my sight?
Whom would you flee? Why show an angry face?
You cannot know from whom I draw my race!
My mother's beauty (and her name) are thine;   15
My sire, Apollo's self, once herded kine.   [Piero
These lambs, unnumbered, are his gift to me,
These cows, that roam around Fiesole.
Their milk forever foams within the pail —
Their milk is constant, and will never fail.   20
Mugello's meadows now belong to me,
More wide and rolling than the Nomads' lea.
The Muses bless me with a poet's name
And bind my temples with the laurel's fame.
Myself am known to all the Tuscan train,   25
As "Daphnis" known to every Tuscan swain,
For from my cave I make the country ring
With songs like those that Tityrus would sing.   [Vergil
This handsome lyre, this lyre that now you see,
Apollo's self, my father, gave to me.   30
Should I build walls (like Orpheus) sure and strong
The stones would move and join themselves to song.
See how the heifers jump for very joy!
See how the wildest lay aside annoy!
See how the very oaks incline to hear!   35
See how the forest now approaches near!
You, you alone attempt to turn and flee —
You, you alone will not endure my plea.
Would you could hear the heavy toil I bear
To win the unyielding, the relentless fair: 40
Long nights I've wandered 'neath a chilly star,
Long days, in winter's cold more freezing far;
The savage hill I've wandered, and the grove,
Deep smitten by the cruel dart of love.
My herds are witness, witness, too, my flocks,   45
How oft I made my bed among the rocks!
Come, maiden, of the Tuscans fairest star,
Admire my skill and prowess from afar:
Now would I take the arrow and the bow
To hunt the boar, to hunt the timid doe.   50
But now, your flight arrest, and boldly stay,
Nor close your ears to blandishments, I pray.
My gardens purple violets display,
And whitest lilies blow to greet the day.
The tender grass is softer, fresher seen: 55
My fleecy lambs cavort amid the green.

24

Here, too, the Naiads sport, in waters clear
That crystal flow from year to coming year.
The well-fed bullocks, at the water's brink,
Come to this stream, at close of day, to drink.   60
Here, while the gentle lambs about us play,
We shall recline and sing, this summer's day.
True, Daphne once was to a laurel turned,
To shun the heat with which her lover burned;
And true it is that I must sing the praise   65
Of the Etruscan Pan through all my days;   [Cosimo
But you as well, my darling love, I'll sing,
And with your praise the farthest age shall ring,
How you surpass in Florence every maid —
In beauty foremost and in virtue staid.   70
The valleys soon shall echo with your name,
The woods shall soon acknowledge all your fame.
The mossy fountain and the flowering grove
Shall know the cause and source of Daphnis' love.
And so, the while my goats explore the height,   75
Your fame shall spread triumphant day and night!"

* * *

By now the folding star began to shine,
To warn the shepherd of the fading time:
He halted, and at last the Nymph was kind —
To all his wishes and his love inclined.

We turn now from the conventions of urbanely rustic Neo-Latin
pastoral to the equally conventional world of urbanely urban elegy,
as portrayed by Ugolino Verino (*Flametta*, ii, 43):

Though you're the glory of the Tuscan race,
    Displaying every beauty, every grace,
Though fairer still your form than Helen's own,
    Though vanquished yet by Venus' self alone,
Though purest white your skin, as is the snow,   5
    Though none so fair can all of Florence show —
That face! Those locks! In which such beauty lies,
    Apollo's self would yield to you the prize!
Those eyes, that burn and flash with starry fires!
    Those lips, that stir the lover's fond desires!   10
And, though your neck is whiter far than milk,
    Your rosy cheeks more red than scarlet silk,
Though small your mouth, though gleaming white your smile

(Ev'n Juno's self would envy, without guile!) —
Your beauty needs no false, deceptive aid: 15
    Your cheek can blush for joy, for fear can fade!
Your back — so straight! So innocent your face!
    Your arms — so comely! So renowned your grace!
My eyes will sparkle at your bosom's rise,
    Nor flat nor pouting: of a seemly size! 20
The girls of Florence you surpass in height:
    From head to toe you are perfection quite!
In song the very Siren's voice would fail,
    In dance the Graces' skill could not avail!
And jealous Juno covets yet your gait: 25
    But envy harms you not, nor Heaven's hate!
Such and so many charms you can display,
    Jove's self had smiled upon your natal day!
Chaste though she was, Lucretia's vanquished quite,
    Whose modesty (and name) you bear by right. 30
Though blest and beautiful in every way,
    That all may think you happy as the day,
Yet never think *this* lover's suit to scorn,
    Whose love will charm you and whose verse adorn.
If riches draw, he's richer far than all! 35
    Yet riches may be bitterer than gall:
Men still can founder in a sea of gold,
    As did Almeon in the days of old.
If you prefer a noble pedigree,
    Who, pray, more noble than the Medici? 40
Not ancient Rome could with such pride display
    Such merits and such lineage as *they*!
If honour, youth, and beauty draw your mind,
    What honoured youth more beauteous could you find?
No other youth more famous in our time, 45
    No youth more worthy of the poet's rhyme:
Castalian Muses love his spirit strong
    And bless him with the primacy in song.
Now, cruel, will you spurn Lorenzo's plea?
    What heart more worthy of a maid like *thee*? 50
His love is pure: no tongue will harm your fame,
    No whispered rumour will assault your name.

* * *

The resemblances between the two poems are plain enough. On the purely formal side, the Ovidian diction of both is unmistakable: this is no more than natural in Verino's elegiac poem, but is less to be

26

expected in the hexameter eclogue of Naldi, where, despit the Vergilian setting and "plot," the tone, manner, and diction are strongly
reminiscent of the passage in Book I of the *Metamorphoses* of Ovid
in which Apollo pursues Daphne —in case we fail to notice this, Naldi
slyly introduces an actual use of Daphne's name at one point. But in
Ovid there is a strong note of satire— Apollo's words to Daphne are,
in that setting, a very amusing and effective parody of Vergil. It goes
without saying, of course, that there is nothing of parody in Naldi's
courtly poem. It is, in fact, just a bit remarkable that he succeeds in
borrowing from Ovid in this way *without* importing any of the flavour
of parody.

In the one poem, the shepherd urges upon his sweetheart all his
own charms, good qualities, and possessions. This is all but invariable,
of course, in the eclogue in ancient, medieval, and Renaissance times.
The reasons Daphnis urges are almost precisely those urged by Apollo
in the passage of the *Metamorphoses* already mentioned, but, more
important, are the very same as those urged by Verino upon Lucrezia:
his looks (actually, Lorenzo was a pretty homely specimen), his wealth
(sheep and cattle in the one poem, gold in the other), his lineage, and,
as a crowning argument, his abilities as a poet,[7] through which he
will be able to make future ages ring with Lucrezia's praises.

Similarly, Lucrezia's beauties (merely hinted at in the Naldi poem,
explicitly detailed in Verino's elegy) are the very same beauties in
each poem. And one passage in Verino's poem, where the girl's height
is mentioned, determines the reference of *excelso vertice* in line 3 of
Naldi's eclogue. In both poems, too, the manner of identifying the girl
is the same. Naldi's poem says that the Nymph has the same name as
Daphnis' mother — and of course Lorenzo's mother was Lucrezia
Tornabuoni. In the elegiac poem Verino says that the girl has the
modesty as well as the name of the original Lucretia in ancient Rome.

The suggestion that Lucrezia has been cruel (and in fact the actual
word *crudelis*) appears in both poems; she is urged, in almost identical
words, not to scorn her lover's suit; she is assured in both poems
that Lorenzo means no harm to her; both poems proclaim, as did
Niccolò Valori, that her beauty is equalled only by her virtue.

----

[7] I have not managed to work it into either translation, but in both poems
he sings his songs at the mouth of a cave.

I could, I suppose, go on to list more such points of resemblance, but have already said enough to make the point that here we have, in all essentials, the very same poem in two versions — one expressed in the urbanely urban and citified idiom of Ovidian elegy, the other in the urbanely rustic idiom of Ovidianized Vergilian pastoral.

The University of British Columbia   W. LEONARD GRANT

APPENDIX OF LATIN TEXTS:

(a) Naldi de Naldis DAPHNIS: Ecloga prima in Laurentium Me-
dicen, iuvenem clarissimum (this corrected text is based on a
collation of four MSS: Siena, Bibl. Com. degli Intronati, cod. lat.
J. ix. 13; Eton Coll., cod. 157; Paris, Bibl. Nat. nouv. acqu. lat.
476 and anc. fonds lat. 8389):

<blockquote>
Daphnis pastor erat, Nymphae correptus amore,
Arni Naiadum turba quae pulchrior omni
praestabat reliquas excelso vertice Nymphas.
hic puer, in teneram dum formosissimus herbam
ductitat unus oves pastum simasque capellas,   5
ista canens suavi referebat carmina voce:
   Hoc ego commerui (nimium crudelis!) amando,
ut me continuo fugias? sic cerva leonem,
sic fugit agna lupum quotiens videt usque rapacem.
ne timeas oro: meme quid spernis amantem?   10
cui nondum posita crevit lanugine barba,
necdum luteolo pallescunt membra colore
(ni quantum iubet asper amor) <nec> turpis honestam
mi puero faciem, nec ruga senilis aravit.
quem fugis? ah, nescis quo sim de sanguine cretus,   15
unde genus ducam! similis tibi nomine, Nympha,
mater adest; pater est mi pastoralis Apollo.
is quoscunque vides me possedisse iuvencos
iussit, et innumeras Fesulanis montibus agnas:
hinc mihi sive novi, veteris seu copia lactis   20
semper adest; caseo mater mea semper abundat.
sunt mihi praeterea prisci complura Mucelli
pascua, quae Nomadum possint evincere saltus.
adde quod et Musae me iam dixere poetam,
et mihi daphnea cinxerunt tempora fronde.   25
hinc ego sum lauri dictus de nomine "Daphnis"
pastor ab Etruscis: viridi nam doctus in antro
tale vel agresti modulor tibi carmen avena
dicere quale solet divino Tityrus ore.
insuper, hace cithara meme donavit Apollo,   30
</blockquote>

"qua "mihi "Dircaeo si condere moenia ritu
percupias" dixit "modulis fidibusque canoris,
in numerum lapides iterum coniungere possis."
nonne vides cantu tauros gestire feroces?
nonne feras sentis quam mitia sumere corda?   35
en, durae nostro flectuntur carmine quercus!
mollitae numeris respondent plurima silvae!
tu tamen una fugis, nec verba precantia curas.
o, saltem libeat nostros audire labores,
quos ego sustineo te propter, diva, nefandos!   40
namque dies memini longos sub sidere Cancri
trivisse et longas brumali frigore noctes,
dum subeo montesque feros atque invia lustra
protinus inquiro, graviori concitus oestro.
testis enim nobis armentum, testis ovile,   45
saepe quod in silvis tenebra veniente tetendi.
huc ades, o virgo, <Tyrrheni> prima fluenti:
iam iuvat incinctae me sumere tela Dianae,
atque acres torquere feras, aprosque feroces
cominus iniectis venari saepe sagittis.   50
siste gradum, precor! hoc tantum patiaris — amari,
et precibus nostris placidas neu clauseris aures!
sunt mihi luteolo violae rubroque colore;
candida praeterea viridi sunt lilia fronde;
hic lentae salices frondent; hic mollior herba   55
et viret et teneros pascit cum matribus agnos.
Naiades hoc Nymphae nitido quoque fonte natare
saepe solent, petra Medicum qui manat ab alta.
hic errant pingues per mollia prata iuvenci;
huc potum veniunt Terzollae ad flumina pasti.   60
hic ubi prospectum nequeunt amittere nostrum,
fluminis ad ripas alterna sorte canamus:
in laurum dices veluti Peneïa virgo
versa est ut castum servaret casta pudorem;
at mihi materia est Etruscum dicere Pana.   65
hinc tu, Nympha, mei certissima causa furoris,
suscipies quantas nostro de carmine laudes!
namque canam Tuscas superes ut sola puellas,
non tantum forma, sed casto insignis honore.
ipse canam: pulsae referent tua nomina valles.   70
ut neque iam caespes, nec iam virgulta, nec ipsi
muscosi fontes, nec circum flumina ripae

ipsa mei valeant causam nescire furoris.
sic, loca dum simae carpent abrupta capellae,
cantibus et cithara semper celebrabere nostra.   75
   Diceret haec Daphnis cum iam lucentibus astris,
pastas ad stabulum cupiens duxisse capellas,
constitit, ex illoque dedit se Nympha videndam
pastori, quoniam tantum spectare cupisset.

(b) Ugolini Verini Flametta, ii, 43: Ad Lucretiam Donatam, ut
     Laurentium Medicem amet (this corrected text is based on four
     MSS: Brit. Mus. Addit. MS 16426; Flor., Magl. VII. 601; Laur.
     Ashburnh. 1703; Laur. plut. XXXIX. cod. 42):

Gloria sis quamvis Tuscae, Lucretia, gentis,
   aequiperesque ipsas nobilitate deas,
nec tua Tyndaridi concedat forma Lacaenae,
   aethereo tantum fulget in ore decus,
sis nive candidior, sis formosissima tota,   5
   exstet ut in toto pulchrius orbe nihil,
sis facie insignis quamvis et crine soluto
   ipse tuis pulcher cedat Apollo comis,
sidereas quamvis vincant tua lumina flammas,
   et tua sint astris aemula labra poli,   10
vincat ebur nitidum quamvis tua lactea cervix,
   et superent roseae punica mala genae,
os minimum dentesque pares candore micantes,
   et risum Iuno vellet habere tuum,
et Tyrio niveus perfusus rideat ostro   15
   vultus, nativus sit color usque genis,
et planae scapulae nihil ut sit rectius illis,
   bracchia non tacta candidiora nive,
parva mamillarum niveo sit pectore, forma,
   nec nimium pinguis nec maculenta nimis,   20
Tyrrhenas collo superes tenus usque puellas,
   nullaque ad exiguos vertice menda pedes,
et quamvis victae cedant tibi voce Sirenae,
   et Charites choreis, cedat et ipsa Venus,
sit roseo vultu divina infusa venustas,   25
   fecerit ut manibus Iuppiter ipse suis,
incessusque tuos quamvis soror ipsa Tonantis,
   denique quicquid habes vellet habere tui,

31

atque pudicitiae exemplar Lucretia cedat,
    cuius habes nomen moribus <ipsa> tuis,   30
et quamvis omni penitus sis parte beata,
    ut te felicem quisque vocare queat,
non tamen idcirco talem contemnere amantem
    debes, sed magis hic ultro petendus erat.
si te divitiae capiunt, ditissimus hic est,   35
    divitias (moneo) nulla puella velit :
divitiis periere viri, periere puellae ;
    Almeonis mater testis avara mihi est.
si te nobilitas titulis insignis avorum
    tangit, quis Medice est nobilitate prior?   40
non fuit in populo generosior ulla Quiritum
    stirps, neque tam claris nobilitata viris.
si mores, si forma placet iuvenilis et aetas,
    iudice te, iuvenis pulcher et ipse probus.
quin age, non alius tota praestantior urbe   45
    est iuvenis, si non saevus adesset Amor.
hunc quoque Castaliis Musae nutriere sub antris,
    et totum hunc fovit Calliopea sinu.
nunc, saeva, immiti patieris amore perire?
    et quis te iuvenis dignior alter <erit>?   50
his te dilexit salvo, Donata, pudore,
    et famam laesit fabula nulla tuam.

Robert Burton, Anglican Minister

B URTONIAN CRITICISM has, strangely enough, paid too little
attention to Burton the divine. Burton the melancholy man,
Burton the recluse, Burton the pillager of dusty old tomes, Burton
the robust and cheerful pessimist have all been studied at the expense
of Burton the compassionate Anglican minister. There is no question
that he is all that the various studies have suggested he is, but he is
much more. His religious commitment remained always a significant
influence in his life and thought; and it is the sincere expression of a
sensitive, competent minister which informs the true spirit of *The
Anatomy of Melancholy.*

Knowledge of Burton's activities as a minister is scarce, and one
cannot push too far the case for him as an influential English church-
man. Aside from his duties at Christ Church where he served as tutor
and college librarian, he held at one time or another three livings:
he was made Vicar of St. Thomas in Oxford, 1616; he served as
Rector of Walesby in Lincolnshire from 1624-1631; and about 1635
he was given the living of Seagrave, where according to Anthony à
Wood, he served "with much ado until his dying day." Despite the
paucity of evidence concerning his clerical activities, Burton's dedication
to helping his unfortunate fellow-men emerges clearly in the *Anatomy.*

Like material in other sections of the *Anatomy*, Burton's thoughts
on religion are strikingly unoriginal. As he did on numerous other
questions, Burton advocates a middle way in religion; and as an
Anglican minister he assumes the role of peacemaker in the struggle
concerning high church ceremonies on the one hand and Calvinistic
dogma on the other which raged in the Anglican Communion during
the first half of the seventeenth century. While other ministers of the
period stressed God's power, Burton stressed His mercy. While others

preached the terrors of sin and reprobation, Burton proposed a humble submission to the will of God.

The best statement of Burton's religious position is that by Lawrence Babb:

Burton's Christianity is emotional and ethical rather than logical or theological. He does not feel altogether at home among abstractions. He is little interested in God's eternity, omnipotency, and immutability but has a great deal to say about His beauty, His love, and His mercy. He endeavors earnestly to confirm in his reader the faith which is necessary to salvation, and through many pages of his book, gently and movingly urges penitence and obedience to the will of a merciful and loving God ... He seems to find the will of God especially in the Two Commandments. ... Other Christian virtues which Burton preaches are submission and patience. ... Although he is doubtless well acquainted with the major Christian controversies, Burton gives scanty attention to disputed theological questions. He has little or nothing to say concerning transubstantiation, the Trinity, faith and works, justification, apostolic succession, or resurrection and judgment. He says strangely little about the after life, nothing at all about the joys of Paradise. [1]

It is Burton's insistence upon the necessity of man's continuous faith in God which characterizes "Religious Melancholy." He ranges far in his examination of those who dismiss God entirely or those presumptuous few who rest upon the doctrine of private revelation. Dismissing both extremes, Burton proposes sincere meditation upon God's beauty and mercy:

... if heauen be so faire, the sun so faire, how much fairer shall he be, that made them faire. ... But for us that are Christians, regenerate, that are his adopted sonnes, illuminated by his word, hauing the eyes of our hearts and vnderstandings opened, how fairely doth he offer and expose himselfe? (I. 1. pp. 7, 9). [2]

"Religious Melancholy" is essentially a sermon and as such it is intended by Burton to be an antidote to the type of preaching prevalent in the seventeenth century:

[1] Lawrence Babb, *Sanity in Bedlam* (East Lansing, 1959), p. 86.
[2] All references to "Religious Melancholy" are from "Robert Burton's *The Anatomy of Melancholy*: 'Religious Melancholy,' A Critical Edition," ed. Dennis G. Donovan, unpublished doctoral dissertation, University of Illinois, 1965.

This meditation terrifies these poore distressed soules, especially if their bodies be predisposed by melancholy, they religiously giuen, & haue tender consciences, euery small obiect affrights them, the very inconsiderate reading of Scripture it selfe, and misinterpretation of some places of it, *as many are called few are chosen. Not euery one that saith Lord.* ... These and the like places terrifie the soules of many, election, predestination, reprobation, preposterously conceaued offend diuerse, with a deale of foolish presumption, curiosity, needlesse speculation, contemplation, sollicitude, wherein they trouble & pussle themselues about those questions of grace, freewill, perseuerance, Gods secrets, they will know more then is revealed by God in his word, humane capacity, or ignorance can apprehend, and too importunate enquiry of that which is revealed, mysteries, ceremonies, obseruations of Sabbaoths, lawes, duties, &c. ... But the greatest harme of all proceedes from those thundering Ministers, a most frequent cause they are of this malady: *and doe more harme in the Church saith Erasmus then they that flatter; great danger on both sides, the one lulles them asleepe in carnall securitie, the other driues them to despaire.* ... But these men are wholy for iudgement, of a rigid disposition themselves, there is no mercy with them no saluation, no balsome for their diseased soules, they can speake of nothing but reprobation, hell, fire and damnation, as they did, *Luke* 11.46. lade men with burdens grieuous to be borne, which they themselues touch not with a finger. (II. 3. pp. 262, 264)

This lengthy passage illustrates clearly, I think, Burton's general attitude toward many of the controversial doctrines of his day; and although he did, as Lawrence Babb suggests, make "a small contribution to the wordy and angry debate concerning predestination," (Babb, p. 87) his general contribution to the doctrinal arguments of the day is infinitesimal.

What is more significant, however, in the passage quoted is Burton's concern with "thundering ministers." It is often they rather than the religious beliefs they represent that lead their parishioners astray, as they bellow forth from the pulpit lurid tales of sins and sinners:

'Tis familiar with our Papists to terrifie mens soules with Purgatorie tales, visions, apparitions, to daunt euen the most generous spirits, to *require Charitie,* as *Brentius* obserues, *of others, bounty, meekenesse, loue, patience, when they themselues breath nought, but lust, enuie, couetousnes.* They teach others to fast, giue almes, doe pennance, & crucifie their mind with superstitious obseruations, bread and water, haire clothes, whippes and the like, when they themselues haue all the dainties the world can afford, lie on a Downe bed, with a curtisan in their armes. (II. 3. p. 264)

35

It is not only the Catholic priest whom Burton attacks for his pulpit conduct; he criticizes also those rigid ministers of his own religion who preach only reprobation and who waste their time on idle controversies:

Our indiscret pastors many of them come not farre behind, whilest in their ordinary sermons they speake so much of election, predestination, reprobation, *ab aeterno,* subtraction of grace, preterition, voluntary permission, &c. by what signes and tokens they shall decerne and try themselues, whether they be Gods true children elect, *an sint reprobi, praedestinati,* &c. with such scrupulous pointes, they still aggrauate sinne, thunder out Gods iudgments without respect, intempestiuely raile at & pronounce them damn'd in all auditories, for giuing so much to sports and honest recreations, making every small fault and thing indifferent an irremissible offence they so rent, teare and wound mens consciences, that they are allmost mad, and at their wits ends. (II. 3. p. 266)

From Burton's comments on the subject, it would appear that the minister's primary duty is to console, not to condemn, and that one's religion should be comforting and attractive. For Burton as for Sir Thomas Browne, the Anglican Church satisfied these qualifications. Again, we might note Babb's observation:

His opinions on Church government and on ceremonial worship seem to align him with the Laudian conservatives. Yet doctrinally he stands with the moderate Calvinistic Puritans. His infrequent references to Calvin are all deferential. He attacks many sects with wrath and ridicule, but never the Presbyterians. He has read, apparently with considerable respect, works by various Puritan divines, notably William Perkins, Richard Geenham and John Downame. These he finds useful especially in his comfort for the despairing conscience. Since he is mildly Calvinistic and Puritanical, his position among early Sturt clergymen is somewhere near the middle point between the two extremes. [3]

As has already been suggested, Burton's Christianity is emotional rather than logical; and at no time do we find him as emotional and as illogical as when he is discussing the religious aberrations of the Papists, the Jews, the followers of Mahomet, and the various separatist sects. If Burton's disposition did not incline him toward quarrelsome disputation, it did not restrain him from attacking what he saw as the work of the devil: the excesses of various religions. Again it should

[3] Babb, p. 90.

be noted that Burton says little that is new on the subject; as usual, he reflects the general tenor of contemporary views.

It must be remembered that to seventeenth-century England, Catholicism was as much a political as a religious threat. As one writer on Burton, William Mueller, has suggested, "the Pope was not seen in competition with the Archbishop of Canterbury but rather with all Protestant monarchs." [4] Still fresh in the minds of many Englishmen were the memories of the Marian persecutions, the debacle of the Spanish Armada, the Gunpowder Plot of 1605, and the attempt of the clever Gondomar to marry the heir-apparent Charles to the Spanish Infanta. It is against such a background of distrust and hatred that Burton's comments on the Catholic Church must be considered. To Burton, as to the other English controversialists who attacked the Catholics, it was the temporal power of the Pope which was their chief concern. And it was upon the Jesuits that they heaped their strongest ridicule, for to them the Jesuits represented the temporal arm of the Papacy. It was the Jesuits who imitated Machiavelli rather than Christ:

Had he [Democritus] more particularly examined a Jesuits life amongst the rest, he should have seen an hypocrite professe povertie, and yet possesse more goods & lands then many princes, to haue infinite treasures and revenues; teach others to fast, and play the gluttons themselves; like watermen, that rowe one way, and look another. ... Monkes by profession, such as give over the world, and the vanities of it, and yet a *Machiavilian* rout interested in all matter of state: holy men, peace makers, and yet composed of envie, lust, ambition, hatred and malice, firebrands, *adulta patriae pestis*, traitors, assasinats, *hac itur ad astra*, and this is to supererogate, and merit heaven for themselues and others. ("Democritus to the Reader," p. 29 [1651])

The Jesuits, as one might expect, do not receive all of Burton's criticism. A large share of it he reserves for their spiritual leader, the Pope. Quoting from Sandys, Burton repeats the "common proverbe":

> *The worst Christians of Italy are the Romans,*
> *of the Romans the Priests are wildest, the*
> *leudest priests are preferred to be cardinalls*

[4] William Mueller, *The Anatomy of Robert Burton's England* (Berkeley and Los Angeles, 1952), pp. 67-68.

> & *the baddest man amongst the Cardinalls is*
> *chosen to be Pope.* (I. 2. p. 67)

As one writer has suggested, "Burton obviously recognized a hierarchical structure!"[5]

The Jews do not escape Burton's censure; and again, it is the superstition of their beliefs which he attacks:

In this superstitious roe, Iewes for antiquity may goe next to *Gentiles* ... for the present, I presume no nation vnder heauen can bee more sottish, ignorant, blinde, superstitious, wilfull, obstinate and peeuish, tiring themselues with vaine ceremonies to no purpose. (I. 3. p. 152)

As a fitting conclusion to Burton's attack upon superstitious religious beliefs, one can find no more appropriate passage than his criticism of the "Mahometans":

Mahometans are a compound of *Gentiles, Iewes,* and *Christians,* & so absurd in their ceremonies, as if they had taken, that which is most sottish out of euery one of them, full of idle fables in their superstitious law, their *Alcoran* it selfe a gallimafery of lies, tales, ceremonies, traditions, precepts, stolne from other sects, and confusedly heaped vp to delude a company of rude and barbarous clownes. (I. 3. pp. 154, 156)

In the seventeenth century the Church of England faced the challenge of Catholicism and the Papacy; but even from within the ranks of Protestantism, the Anglican Church was challenged by the separatist sects. If the Catholic Church was dangerous for its dogmatic insistence upon rites and ceremonies, the separatist sects were just as dangerous for their insistence upon the stripping away of all tradition. We have seen how Burton responded to the threat of the Papacy, but we should also note his censure of those who would destroy in an instant, Christian traditions and symbols:

But see the Diuell that will neuer suffer the Church to be quiet or at rest. No Garden so well tilled, but some noxious weedes growe vp in it, no wheat but it hath some tares, we haue a madde giddy company of precisians, Schismaticks, and some Heretickes euen in our owne bosomes in another extreame, *Dum vitant stulti vitia in contraria currunt.* That out of too much zeale, in

---

[5] Mueller, p. 75.

ROBERT BURTON

opposition to Antichrist, humane traditions, those Romish rites and superstitions, will quite demolish all, they will admit of no ceremonies at all, no fasting dayes, no crosse in Baptisme, kneeling at Communion, no Church musicke, &c. (I. 3. p. 178)

We find in Burton's religious thought then, two concepts (comfort for the distressed soul and hatred for other religious sects) seemingly at variance with each other. But it must be remembered that Burton is attacking only the excesses of other religious beliefs, excesses which are after all, in Burton's thinking, not the manifestation of God's spirit, but the work of the devil in his never-ending effort to delude man.

Although it may seem that Burton the masterful investigator of abnormal psychology often dismisses the world and all in it with the comment "All is Mad," more frequent and more typical is an exhortation such as the following by Burton the minister:

If Satan summon thee to answer, send him to Christ, he is thy liberty, thy protector against cruell death, raging sinne, that roaring Lion, he is thy righteousnes, thy Sauiour, and thy life. Though he say thou art none of the number of the elect, a reprobate, forsaken of God, hold thine own still, — *hic murus ahenius esto,* let this be as a bulwarke, a brazen wall to defend thee, stay thy selfe in that certainty of faith; let that be thy comfort, Christ will protect thee, vindicate thee, thou art one of his flock, he will triumph ouer the Law, vanquish death, ouercome the Diuell, and destroy hell. (II. 6. pp. 326-327)

Despite his bookishness, and his seclusion from the theater of common life, Burton's concern in the *Anatomy* is man and his myriad problems. The *Anatomy* is a testament to man in all his strength and weakness.

University of North Carolina   DENNIS G. DONOVAN

Sir Roger de Trumpington (Trumpington, Cambridgeshire)

A French Humanist's Chef-D'Oeuvre: The Commentaries on Seneca's *"De Clementia"* by John Calvin

TODAY, A YOUNG scholar, anxious to achieve immediate acclaim as an authority in his field, probably thinks in terms of receiving a Doctorate, locating a post at an Ivy League institution, and publishing a book. In the era of the Renaissance the requisites for admittance to the inner circle of scholars were not exactly the same —Erasmus, for example, was never anything more than a visiting professor at an institution of higher learning— but the publication of an erudite study of classical theme was an almost sure-fire method of attracting the attention of established authors and assuring one's entrance into the world of the literati. It has not been definitely ascertained why John Calvin, in 1532, wrote his *Commentaries on Seneca's "De Clementia."* Earlier historians, such as Papire Masson, Guizot, Henry, and Pannier saw in Calvin's work a plea to Francis I to show mercy in his dealings with Protestants, [1] and even Émile Doumergue in his monumental classic, *Jean Calvin, Les Hommes et les Choses de son Temps,* echoed that theory. More recent studies such as those by Quirinus Breen, Basil Hall, or Ford Battles have suggested an entirely different explanation. They see Calvin, not as a Protestant reformer in that period of his life, but as a humanist à la Erasmus or Budé who thus designed his work on Seneca to be a humanist's chef-d'œuvre which would transform the author overnight, as it were, into a master of repute. However, there is still a general tendency among those who write of Calvin to ignore entirely, or almost entirely, his career as humanist and, specifically, his *Com-*

---

[1] The *De Clementia* was addressed by Seneca to the young emperor Nero to urge him to be merciful in his relations with his subjects.

mentaries on Seneca and their significance as a preparation for Calvin the Reformer. M. Lecoultre had commented on this in an article appearing in 1891 and noted that the *Commentaries* had never been translated from Latin [2] — they still have not. Professor Basil Hall remarked that it is a well-known fact that Calvin's effect was so earth-shaking as to transform "the religion of half Western Europe." Yet people fail to realize that Calvin was a "humanist lawyer before he was a theologian." [3]

What is the evidence which would indicate that Calvin was a humanist, at least until the fall of 1533? First, it has been demonstrated that Calvin's training was humanistic, his interests were inclined in that direction, his motive for writing the *Commentaries* was in keeping with the typical aspirations and conduct of a humanist, and finally, the work itself was a typical Renaissance study of the North of Europe.

Calvin, as most students of the Reformation must be aware, was sent in August of 1523 to the College of La Marche at Paris where he received excellent instruction in Latin and French under the humanist, Mathurin Cordier. Later, but in the same year, Calvin transferred to the College of Montaigu where instruction was thorough and where a professor of some note, the Scottish nominalist, John Major or Mair, lectured. Finally, it was here that religious liberals, such as Roussel, Olivétan, and Nicholas Cop, the son of Francis I's physician, were to become his friends. [4]

In 1528, Calvin's studies at the University were interrupted by his father's decision that his son's career lay in the study of law rather than theology. This choice may not have been a second-best one, as far as the father was concerned. Calvin, later, in his *Commentary on the Psalms* asserted that his father chose that profession for him on the basis of its profit-making expectancies. At any rate, Calvin went first to the University of Orléans and, later (the following year), to that of Bourges to study. [5] One of those who influenced him strongly at Orléans was Melchior Wolmar who taught him Greek, and Calvin also found a friend in François Daniel with whom he corresponded later with regard

[2] H. Lecoultre, *Calvin d'après son "Commentaire sur le 'De Clementia' de Sénèque (1532)* (Lausanne, 1891), p. 4.
[3] Basil Hall, *John Calvin: Humanist and Theologian* (London, 1956), p. 7.
[4] *Ibid.*, p. 9.   [5] *Ibid.*, p. 11.

to the Seneca *Commentaries*, [6] as well as Nicholas Duchemin, whose *Antapologia* would contain a preface composed by Calvin. [7] Furthermore, Calvin studied under Pierre Taisan de l'Estoile, the most noted instructor of law. This training, Professor Breen maintains, provided Calvin with "the background for appreciating the critical work of Budé and ... Alciati." [8] In 1529 Calvin, now having enrolled at the University of Bourges, continued his study of law under Andrea Alciati, the only Italian instructor that Calvin was to have, who had "brought with him the atmosphere of the trans-Alpine Renaissance." [9]

In 1531, on the death of his father, Calvin returned to Paris to study at the Royal College (Lecteurs Royaux), [12] an institution where lectureships in Latin, Greek, and Hebrew were available. Here Calvin would attend classes in Greek taught by Pierre Danès, a humanist, and one in Hebrew taught by François Vatable, one of the most prominent Renaissance figures in France. [13] Soon Calvin in April 1532, published his first work, his *Commentaries on Seneca's "De Clementia."* [14] His strongly humanist background would explain, not only his interest in classical authors, but his familiarity with and interest in contemporary humanist writers. Thus, Calvin had chosen Seneca over other classical authors on the advice of Erasmus who, in the preface of his second edition of the works of Seneca published in 1529, had written that further editorial comments on Seneca by young scholars were welcomed. [15] Did Calvin believe that if he accepted the challenge offered by the "Prince of Humanists," who had thus placed his stamp of approval upon the name and thought of Seneca, he would be accorded an eager reception by the community of famous writers? It seems so; however, another explanation has been offered — the fact that during the Renaissance there occurred a revival of Stoicism, a philosophy which tends naturally to become attractive in troubled times. Professor Breen sug-

---

[6] Quirinus Breen, *John Calvin: A Study in French Humanism* (Grand Rapids, Michigan, 1931), pp. 40-43.

[7] *Ibid,,* p. 37.

[8] *Ibid.,* p. 43.

[9] *Ibid.,* pp. 44-46.

[12] Hall, p. 12.

[13] Breen, pp. 62-63.

[14] *Ibid.,* p. 65.

[15] The earlier edition of Seneca's works, the one of 1515, appeared under the name of Erasmus, but the latter disclaimed the honor of having undertaken that task by explaining that only the preface was his. The job of publication was that of a friend. See Lecoultre, p. 6.

gests, too, that Stoicism may have been revived as a counterforce against the growing popularity of another Hellenistic philosophy, Epicureanism. Humanists in France fell into various classifications, but those who belonged to the cult of Erasmus were fond of searching the classics, especially the writings of the Stoics, as Cicero or Seneca, for instruction in moral law. In this circle would also be found those who, like Calvin, were students of Roman civil law. [16] But what of the theory that the *Commentaries* were written in order to recommend Protestants to the mercy of Francis I? There is no evidence to support such a view. Nowhere is the French King given mention; the work is not even dedicated to him, and, as M. Lecoultre points out, for Calvin to have compared Francis with Nero, to whom Seneca addressed his work, would have been a gross miscalculation. Francis, at that time, was not given over to persecutions. Neither is there anything of a specific nature that might be described as Protestant. [17] As Professor Breen shows, Calvin could not have been interested in Protestantism at that time. [18] Did Calvin, himself, provide any clue to his decision to produce the *Commentaries?* All that appears is a very brief explanation in his dedicatory letter in which he lamented the fact that Seneca, although he enjoyed the reputation of being one of the best writers of classical Rome, had not proved especially popular in Calvin's day. Therefore, he (Calvin) had looked forward for some time to the coming of a famous champion of Seneca's name. [19] Theodore Beza (Bèze), later to be Calvin's successor in Geneva and the author of a biography of him, had merely this to offer: soon after the death of his father, Calvin returned to Paris where he wrote his commentary on Seneca, "a great favorite with him (Beza)" because he was "obviously in accord with Calvin." [20]

Was there any reason why Calvin, when he returned to Paris in 1531, should have chosen to attend the Royal College rather than the

---

[16] Hall, p. 7.   [17] Lecoultre, p. 24.

[18] Breen, p. 80.

[19] Jean Calvin, *L. Annaei Senecae...libro duo De Clementia...Jo. Calvini Noviodunaei Commentariis illustrati...* in *Ioannis Calvini Opera quae supersunt omnia*, eds. Guilielmus Baum, Eduardus Cunitz, Eduardus Reuss, vol. V (Brunswick, 1863-1900) in *Corpus Reformatorum*, vol. LV, p. 7. This is hereafter cited as *Comm.*

[20] John Calvin, *Tracts relating to the Reformation by John Calvin with His Life by Theodore Beza*, trans. Henry Beveridge (Edinburgh, 1844), vol. I, p. xxiv.

University of Paris? Since the Sorbonne by 1526 had begun its condemnation of "dangerous" books, including the writings of Erasmus, only one answer seems likely. Calvin must have been a humanist, and in keeping with the sentiment of other humanists, preferred to shun the University of Paris and attend lectures delivered by humanist professors in a college founded through the efforts of Budé, the foremost French humanist, to combat the conservative tendencies of the scholastics of Paris. [21] Therefore, Calvin in 1532 could hardly have been a Protestant, but a young man of the Renaissance seeking to make his mark in the world.

Any examination of the *Commentaries* makes it clear that we have before us the kind of classical study which an Erasmus or a Budé would have produced. First of all, Calvin revealed that he was a Latinist of a superb order, as he explained and analyzed Seneca's *De Clementia* from the standpoint of grammar, philosophy, and history. [22] Furthermore, Calvin displayed in this work a wide range of knowledge of Greek and Roman classical authors, as well as an acquaintance with other humanist writings of his day. What is more, Calvin expressed his approval and praise of such secular writings. Professor Ford Battles, who has made a study of the sources used by Calvin in his *Commentaries,* has shown that Cicero was cited more often than any other author; there are approximately sixty references to his *Letters,* ninety five to the *Speeches,* eighteen to the rhetorical writings, and eighty to his philosophical treatises. [23] However, Calvin also referred to Horace, Juvenal, Lucan, Ovid, Plautus, Terrence, Virgil, Suetonius, Tacitus, Plutarch, Livy, Sallust, and others. [24]

Special eulogies were paid by Calvin to two contemporary humanists, Budé and Erasmus. The former was described as the "first glory and support of literary affairs, thanks to whom our France claims today the palm of erudition"; [25] it is his *Annotations* which have revealed to us what is "equitable and good." [26] On the other hand, Erasmus, heralded elsewhere as the chief of humanists, was rated as second-best, although still one of the "first delights" of the realm of letters. [27] It

[21] See Breen, p. 35. [22] *Ibid.,* p. 14.
[23] Ford Battles, "The Sources of Calvin's Seneca Controversy," *John Calvin,* ed. Gervase Duffield (Appleford, Abingdon, Berkshire, 1966), p. 49.
[24] *Ibid.,* p. 53. [25] *Comm.,* p. 54.
[26] *Ibid.,* p. 119. [27] *Ibid.,* p. 6.

has been ably demonstrated by Professors Battles and Breen that of these two, it was Budé who exerted the greater degree of influence upon Calvin in that his (Budé's) *Annotations on the Pandects of Justinian* provided Calvin with the technical terms and concepts of Roman law, as well as other aspects of Roman society, for Calvin believed that to understand the *De Clementia* he needed an understanding of the whole of Roman history, and, more specifically, the history of the reign of Nero. [28] Professor Breen also suggests that another influence upon Calvin must have been derived from Budé's *L'institution du Prince* which consists of apophthegms from Plutarch's work of that name which, as was true of the *De Clementia,* offered advice to a young king. Thus, this work and Calvin's *Commentaries* had essentially the same purpose, and it is interesting to note that the first sentence of Calvin's *Commentaries* came from the apophthegms of Plutarch. [29]

Calvin also utilized a work by another humanist, this time an Italian, Lorenzo Valla, who in his *Elegantiae,* had laid the foundations of modern classical philology. That Calvin should be impressed by Valla's work is not surprising, especially in the light of Budé's recommendation of him in his *Annotations.* [30]

Professor Battles indicates one more contemporary influence on Calvin, that of Philippus Beroaldus the Elder, whose Commentaries on Suetonius' *Lives of the Caesars* were studied closely by Calvin. [31]

As for Erasmus, there are several references by Calvin to the *Adagia,* one to the Panegyric of Philip, and it is highly probable that Calvin was familiar with the *Education of a Christian Prince.* [32]

Though under the spell of classical letters and the thought of contemporary humanists, Calvin demonstrated his mettle as a humanist scholar in his own right by the painstaking and exacting manner in which he carried through his task of explaining and expounding the ideas of Seneca. Here also, Calvin displayed the marks of a questioning spirit by his refusal to swallow whole the philosophy of Seneca. However, this was not all. Even the great Budé and Erasmus were not spared his critical eye; nor were the judicial and educational systems of his time immune from attack. For example, Calvin, taking exception

---

[28] See Breen, pp. 119-120 and Battles, pp. 42-45.
[29] Breen, p. 120. [31] Battles, pp. 46-47.
[30] *Ibid.,* p. 104. [32] *Ibid.,* pp. 40-41.

to Erasmus' acrimonious assault in his preface of 1529 upon some of the ethical and religious beliefs of Seneca, as well as his literary merits,[33] rose to Seneca's defense in the Preface to his *Commentaries* by praising him as "a man of great erudition and of remarkable eloquence . . .; the first after Cicero, he is a pillar of philosophy and Roman eloquence."[34]

Hereafter, Calvin referred only rarely to "errors" of Erasmus in interpretation and word-usage.[35] In several passages, however, Calvin continued to exhibit this critical tendency in his attacks upon the venality of the judges of his day[36] and in his censure of teachers whom he termed "cruel tyrants" to whom the name "pedagogue" would be an insult.[37] Even Seneca was not allowed to escape reproof. Calvin decried his verbosity, absence of order, and his occasional inaccuracies in historical references.[38] Calvin was also prepared to reject any thoughts which were not in harmony with his own religious or ethical convictions. Thus, Seneca's references to the operation of Fortune or Chance prompted Calvin to remark that he (Seneca) should have written, "Providence."[39] The impersonal clemency extolled by Seneca appalled him also, and, in support of his own position, he cited St. Augustine and Cicero.[40] In another commentary Calvin reproved Seneca for declaring that he was not preoccupied with the thought of his reputation, but was content with the witness of his conscience.[41] And when Seneca referred to souls which are "ambitious," Calvin raised an objection to the use of the word, "ambitious." "Here, Seneca," Calvin commented, "shows clearly what those eminent virtues of the pagans were."[42] Thus, to Calvin the virtues of the ancients were tainted with the evils of self-centeredness and vain-glory.

Such evidences of a critical disposition in Calvin were in keeping with the mood of the Renaissance, but, alas, the thrusts of a young unknown against the great Erasmus, mild though they were, may have been regarded amiss, and could well have proved responsible, or partly responsible, for the failure of Calvin's first publication to reach the best-seller list of the day.

---

[33] See Lecoultre, p. 7.
[34] *Comm.*, pp. 6-7.
[35] See *Ibid.*, pp. 32, 159.
[36] *Ibid.*, p. 23.
[37] *Ibid.*, p. 115.

[38] *Ibid.*, p. 7.
[39] *Ibid.*, p. 18.
[40] *Ibid.*, pp. 156-157.
[41] *Ibid.*, pp. 111-112.
[42] *Ibid.*, p. 45.

It should be kept in mind, however, that Calvin's censures were infrequent, and, when they occurred, delivered in a courteous and somewhat apologetic manner. [43] As might be expected of a book authored by a humanist, eulogies of classical antiquity and contemporary scholarship abounded. Generally speaking, Seneca's advice to the Emperor Nero was viewed favorably, and, as we have seen, Erasmus and especially Budé, were accorded lavish praise.

What was the political theory of Seneca which attracted the attention of young Calvin? First of all, Seneca's prince —and Calvin's too— is absolute in power — for in the *Commentaries* Seneca is quoted as maintaining the principle that the emperor's powers are subject to no law save that of the gods, and Calvin echoes this proposition by declaring that the prince is indeed free of the law and responsible alone to divine authority. It must be added, however, that Calvin does modify this principle somewhat, for he states that it would be better for the well-being of the state or people if the ruler submits to the law instead of placing himself over it and refers to a passage in Cicero's *De Officiis* in which the author compares administrators to the protectors of the republic. [44] In another passage Calvin writes that it is the duty of the prince to minister unto the "health and care of men"; of those good things which God has given to them, they distribute a portion to their subjects and a part they retain for themselves. He then proceeds to quote the passage from Romans XIII in which subjects are admonished to obey the powers —that— be. [45] Thus, Calvin attempts to show that there are some postulates which Christians and pagan Stoics share in common.

Of all the qualities possessed by princes none is more impressive in the eyes of Seneca and Calvin than that of clemency. Once again Seneva invokes the principle of natural law to support his contention, for in the natural kingdom, Seneca notes, the ruler of the bees is more impressive than the rest, but has no sting. [46] The human prince should conduct himself in the same manner, since that man is truly great who,

[43] As an illustration of this, Calvin in his Preface (p. 6) stated: "a number of points failed to be observed by Erasmus ... a criticism which may be made without ill-will."

[44] *Comm.*, pp. 23-25.   [45] *Ibid.*, p. 18.

[46] Lucius Annaeus Seneca, *The Stoic Philosophy of Seneca; Essays and Letters of Seneca,* ed. Moses Hadas (Gloucester, Mass., 1965), p. 158.

though wronged and in possession of unlimited power, is able to keep his temper in check and knows the meaning of the word "magnanimous." [47] In another passage, Seneca once more finds a parallel in nature. This time, the cruel king is compared with a stormy day. Since a king finds it easy to take vengeance on those who have offended him, he is to be awarded unqualified praise when he exercises, instead, gentleness and restraint. The king who is, by his very position, elevated above the crowd and hence most apt to be noticed, must be doubly aware of his reputation, for people are watching him. [48] Calvin observes that Seneca's remarks on the restraint which a ruler must exercise indicate that a condition has been imposed on kings. For them, intemperance and license are an abomination. When we refer to the ruled, we may speak of a man's angry disposition, but in the case of a ruler, the harshest terms of disapprobation such as "cruel" and "proud" are in order. [49] In the matter of the dispensation of acts of mercy, Seneca points out that clemency is of value to both the innocent and the guilty; if applied properly it will make a large portion of mankind innocent again. On the other hand, pardon, if general, ends in chaos and an "eruption of vice." Thus, moderation should be employed with the object of separating the "curable from the hopeless." [50] Calvin concurs with this view, [51] and later refers to the picture which Gregory the Great painted in his *Moralia* of the impartial judge who, with scales in hand, extends both justice and compassion. ... Through justice he pronounces the sentence of sin and through compassion he tempers the penalty of sin. ..." [52]

According to Seneca, the clement ruler will discover that his subjects are much more likely to render loyal service to him than would be the case if he attempted to rule as a cruel tyrant. Of the power of a ruler, Seneca wrote, is indeed directed toward promoting the well-being of his subjects, the latter will know that their prince is on their side and will willingly sacrifice their own lives, if need be, in the defense of their monarch. [53] Calvin agrees that clemency is a "heroic virtue without which princes are not able to rule." Such a quality does not

---

[47] *Ibid.*, pp. 159-160.
[48] *Ibid.*, pp. 145-146.
[49] *Comm.*, p. 65.
[50] Seneca, p. 140.

[51] *Comm.*, p. 35.
[52] *Ibid.*, p. 37.
[53] Seneca, p. 141.

constitute a sign of weakness. Indeed, a king may be powerful; it is permissible for him to be so. However, he will discover that if he does not tone down his immoderate actions, affairs of state will not run smoothly. "All things will lose their charm unless he takes upon himself the qualities of gentleness and graciousness. He will then find that all his words and deeds will be accepted without opposition if he has conciliated the favor of the people ... by this virtue (clemency)." [54] In this manner, a king's reign is a stable one if the ruler becomes a "veritable shepherd of his people," ministering to the best interests of those placed in his charge. On the other hand, the prince who rules as a tyrant reaps his own destruction. [55]

Calvin also approved Seneca's assertion that the prince is to the state as the soul is to the body. For as the soul rules over and moderates all functions of the members, so are those placed under the rule of a prince nurtured and guided and governed. [56]

Did the practice of clemency enjoined by Seneca and Calvin mean that the prince must rid himself of rod and sword? Hardly. Seneca and also Calvin were in accord that all men are sinners and that sins need to be punished. Why? Seneca cites three reasons: (1) to reform a man; (2) to set an example for other men; (3) to lock up the criminal so that the rest of society will be protected from him. In the first case, the lighter form of punishment is preferable, believed Seneca. If a man has something worth saving he "will live more heedfully." It is otherwise with the individual who has already lost his reputation. As for the state, it benefits also if sparing use is made of punishment. [57] A ruler's clemency has the effect of making men ashamed of wrong-doing and "punishment seems more grievous if it is inflicted by a kindly man." [58] On the other hand, overly-harsh forms of punishment may lead to outbursts of violent indignation, and Seneca cites, as an example, revolts of private citizens and slaves against those who invoked the extreme penalty of crucifixion. [59] Frequent punishments also lead to internal dissension, for if a king punishes frequently, he may prevent a few from hating him, but the hatred of all is aroused since antagonisms

[54] *Comm.*, p. 41.
[55] *Comm.*, p. 41-42.
[56] *Ibid.*, pp. 42-43.

[57] Seneca, p. 161.
[58] *Ibid.*, p. 162.
[59] *Ibid.*, p. 164.

have a way of multiplying. One execution provokes the many relatives of the executed to become the sworn enemies of the prince. [60]

Another recommendation which Seneca makes is that a state to be moral must be led to think of itself as a good state. He illustrates this by referring to the occasion when a motion was made in the Senate to create a distinctive dress for slaves and freemen, and then the danger of this procedure was realized. The slaves would begin counting the number of freemen. Thus, if no one came to be pardoned, we would soon note that the worst element was in the majority. [61]

Seneca's arguments for light and infrequent punishments were carefully noted and sanctioned by Calvin who deplored the cruel, tyrannical actions of a prince, who, free from all checks upon his authority, gives full reign to the basest of emotions, meting out punishments with the heavy hand of vengeance. [62] Sometimes a king must execute, he maintained, but only when public welfare necessitates it. [63]

Should a ruler fail to heed the advice of Seneca and rule tyrannically, was there no way for his subjects to find release? Was there a theory of right of revolution in the thought of Seneca and Calvin? No, but their propositions led them close to the threshold of Lockeian ratiocination, for it will be recalled that Seneca had observed that a cruel ruler bears within himself the fruits of his own debacle in that revolutions somethimes break out in opposition to the cruel deeds of a despot. Calvin notes that they who are cruel and tyrannical are cursed while they live and are often destroyed by the sword. Subjects may, then, take comfort in the thought that though the rule of a wicked prince may be a 'stormy' one it will also be a brief one. [64]

Seneca sees yet another effect of tyranny. This time it is not the reaction of the populace to deeds of cruelty or the physical harm which may befall a prince that concerns him, but the question of the effect of evil deeds upon the soul of the man who commits them. What are the psychological changes which accompany the tyrant's acts? Seneca paints a picture of the progressive deterioration of a man's character. One crime leads to another and another as the cruel ruler finds that he cannot call a halt to his evil actions. Faces of death are

[60] *Ibid.*, pp. 146-147.
[61] *Ibid.*, p. 162.
[62] See *Comm.*, Book I, chaps. VIII, XXIII and XXIV.
[63] *Ibid.*, p. 104.
[64] *Ibid.*, p. 89.

at every hand and, for once, the ruler knows the meaning of fear, but the new emotion merely leads him on to further acts of violence. Gradually, he reaches the stage where he is unable to trust anyone and is frequently tormented by fears of death, or more often, the desire to die. [65] Calvin adds that tyranny is that "miserable state" which serves only to "horrify both gods and men." [66] And there is also the "mirror of conscience" which reveals that "reflection of the vermin within." [67]

Thus, Calvin observes two results of tyranny: outwardly, revolutions or riotings may occur; and, inwardly, the tyrant becomes, in the end, a sniveling coward afraid to approach his most intimate friends and is filled with a fear of, or even longing for, extinction. In rebelling against the cruel tyrant, the subjects may not be exercising a right of revolution, but they are fulfilling a role which the natural law dictates, for rebellion in the *De Clementia* appears as the natural consequence of the evil deeds of a prince. If in Stoic philosophy, 'virtue is its own reward', then injustice brings its own reward, too — revolutions, and rioting and inner throes of conscience.

Calvin's prince is, thus, a ruler with no limitations upon his own powers save those of his own devising. These self-imposed restraints he has learned to exercise, for he knows that for his own good and the well-being of his state he must rule in justice, temperance, and clemency. Is he not the antithesis of the Renaissance ideal of princehood? Certainly, Calvin's ruler is no Machiavellian prince who has been advised to take upon himself the ways of the fox and lion. Nor has he been told that it is not necessary to be clement and humane; all that is demanded is that he just appear to possess those qualities. On the other hand, Calvin's prince is remarkably similar to the ideal princes which are depicted in Erasmus' *Institutio Principis Christiani* and Budé's *L'Institution du Prince*. In the former work, the prince, just as Calvin's, considers the welfare of his people and shows mercy in dealing with violators of the law. In Budé's book, the ruler is likewise presented as humane and just, as he strives to set a good example for his subjects.

[65] Seneca, p. 153.
[66] *Comm.*, p. 87.

[67] *Ibid.*, p. 102.

Calvin's *Commentaries,* even with respect to their political content, are thus found to be congenial with other political writings which were produced by the Northern Renaissance.

University of Alabama, Huntsville　　　　　LOUISE SALLEY

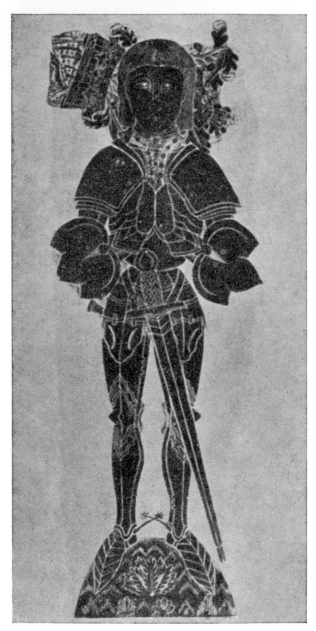

Sir Anthony de Gray (St. Alban's Cathedral)

Character Identification in the Theatre:
Some Principles and Some Examples

S HAKESPEARE SCHOLARSHIP is displaying an increasing concern for the theatrical dimension of Shakespeare's artistry, for what J. L. Styan in characterizing the uniqueness of the genre of drama refers to as "what the text makes the actor make the audience do." [1]

Theatrically oriented interpretation has in recent years supplemented what still remains a classic, Granville-Barker's *Prefaces*. Recognition of the theatrical dimension of Shakespeare's artistry has provided a curb on the excessive intricacy of interpretation resting on singular details and contradicting what is "writ large" in the dramatic story, as illustrated in Nevill Coghill's effective rebuttal to T. S. Eliot's famous reading of Othello's speech in the final scene. [2] Recognition of this theatrical dimension has also provided the proper context for shedding light on problems of apparent magnitude when viewed from the privacy and the rationality of the study; taking seriously the communal, heavily emotional experience of the theatre has produced such healthy observations as that of C. P. Lyons, in his reconstruction of the staging of the first scene of *Antony and Cleopatra*: "Antony and Cleopatra are centered in a stage picture which is framed by his scornful soldiers on one side and the scorned Roman envoys on the other." [3] Recently, such diverse works as Gerald Bentley's *Shakespeare and his Theatre*, Bernard Beckerman's *Shakespeare at the Globe,* Richard Southern's writings, the exciting *Elements of Drama* by J. L. Styan, and at least portions

---

[1] J. L. Styan, *The Elements of Drama* (Cambridge, 1963), p. 2.
[2] Nevill Coghill, *Shakespeare's Professional Skills* (Cambridge, 1964), pp. xiv-xv.
[3] Clifford P. Lyons, "Stage Imagery in Shakespeare's Plays," *Essays on Shakespeare and Elizabethan Drama in Honor of Hardin Craig,* edited by Richard Hosley (Columbia, Mo., 1962), p. 272.

of Nevill Coghill's *Shakespeare's Professional Skills* have demonstrated the value of employing a stage context in dramatic criticism. Besides curbing excesses, clarifying effects, or solving cruxes, a theatrical context is vital to the editor, the critic, and the reader of Shakespeare simply because Shakespeare wrote for the theatre — an obvious tautology but, consequently, a significant one.

I wish here to explore one small corner of "Shakespeare as theatre" and its implications for editor, critic, and reader. This is the matter of Shakespeare's practices in identifying stage personages for his theatre audience, who had, of course, no access to what is so familiar and inescapable to us as readers today — a list of characters, stage-directions, and speech-prefixes which, insofar as possible, use as specific and exact a name as possible for each character.

Fundamentally, my concern is this: (1) precisely how does a theatre audience know, for example, that "he's Hamlet," "she's Countess of Rousillon," "he's Valentine," or "he's Malvolio"? (2) And what visual aspects of a characterization, briefly or infrequently alluded to in the dialogue, are part of the audience's *continual* visual impression of that character? That is, what generic visual considerations, such as the youthfulness of Arthur in *King John,* the deformity of Richard III, or the Moor-ness of Othello (rather than the unique features of a single production, such as brocade, blue, and actor's build) supplement —or substitute for— the audience's appellative recognition of a character? Editors (as well as dramatists and playhouse prompters for efficient use of a script) regularize character identification in the rubrics of a text — that is, in the stage-directions and speech-prefixes. Thus, whether professional critics, students, housewives, or plumbers, readers uniformly identify characters by (*merely*) *names.*

But my two questions suggest that no such uniformity exists in the experience of a theatre audience: despite a name in the published text of *How to Succeed in Business without Really Trying,* my reaction to her in the theatre is that of the proverbial "voluptuous dumb blond secretary." And surely this identification accords with the dramatist's expectation. Likewise in Shakespeare, sometimes the theatrical identification of a character is something *more* —or *less*— than "a name."

Costuming identified the social status and, sometimes, even the vocation of a character immediately. Exact Elizabethan stage costuming cannot be reconstructed, but neither are the details of blue and brocade generic. Dramatic significance rarely resided in such particulars, necessary but variable considerations for different performances of a single play. Malvolio's indecorous, gaudy appearance is an obvious exception, but such instances are, at least from the evidence of the dialogue, rare. Rather, the dramatic significance of costuming in Shakespeare's plays resided in broadly defined contrasts, such as Roman versus Egyptian in *Antony* and king versus courtier versus commoner in the histories and tragedies. And either incidental dialogue references or the entire dramatic situation provides an awareness of such contrasts. Such costuming differences have narrative and fundamental dramatic significance, whereas such particulars as color and material usually influence only the degree of visual sumptuousness of a particular performance.

Incidental dialogue references and the dramatic situation sometimes provide indications of theatrical type, such as "clownish" or "malcontent," which would continually and forcefully be part of the audience's visual experience. The two-dimensional villainy of Don John in *Much Ado* (and possibly his bastardry?) would be immediately and forcefully apparent visually for an audience in 1. 1, although in this scene a reader lacking theatrical imagination knows of such a character —without emotional reactions— from only the opening stage-direction and one line of dialogue. Whereas some readers may only *occasionally* think of Othello's color, in the theatre it is an inescapable consideration whenever Othello is on stage. And in some manner emblematic costuming of Shylock probably pointed up constantly his miserliness, his Jewishness, and/or his Pantaloon-like theatrical conventionality.

But such considerations provide identification only in terms of social status, vocation, dramatic function, or theatrical type. Essentially three other means cooperate to provide the individualizing of a name. First, a person's name could appear in the dialogue at or near his first entrance, either in announcement ("Here comes Signior Claudio...") or direct-address ("That thou, Iago..."). Secondly, dialogue references prior to a character's entrance create anticipation, so that the audience immediately associates a character on entrance with the earlier use of his name. Such foreshadowing assures the prominence of announcement or direct-address appellation. For example, Montague, Lady Montague, and Benvolio's discussion in the first scene centers around the yet unseen "Romeo." And thirdly, the title of a play, together with costuming (and repertory casting practices), could occasionally provide an audience with individualized identification. Knowledge of the title *King Lear,* for example, permitted Shakespeare to assume that an audience would recognize the character attired as a king to be "King Lear" without the usual foreshadowing and entrance announcement of the name of a major character.

Popular editing (which can treat the rubrics, although not the dialogue, with freedom) and criticism should reflect these generic elements of stage presentation which influence Shakespeare's dramaturgy, which are part of the fullest possible understanding of that dramaturgy. And a character's dramatic significance is, to a considerable degree, influenced by the audience's awareness of the character's identity — whether he is memorably known by name from his first entrance or gradually introduced as a unique personality; whether thought of in terms of his name alone or in terms of social status, vocation, relationships to other characters; whether seen in disguise or predominantly in terms of a single visual attribute.

Generally, Shakespeare presents prominently and frequently the name of a major character within the dialogue. The name "Romeo" is known first from the title, then discussion of his whereabouts and condition prior to his first entrance is introduced by "O, where is Romeo," and his entrance breaking up this discussion is announced by "See, where he comes." Romeo's name appears naturally and frequently —at least eighty times— in the conversation of the play. The names of other major characters are also generally prominent and frequent in the dialogue. Macbeth's name is mentioned prior to his entrance — by the witches, the bleeding soldier, and King Duncan. Immediately upon his first entrance, Macbeth is identified by this name which, by then, contains much anticipated interest. In *Much Ado,* the name Claudio appears more than fifty times, and "Benedick," "Hero," and "Beatrice" appear about forty times each. Usually Shakespeare makes the name of a central character prominent for the audience.

58

On the other hand, very minor and supernumerary roles are not usually individualized with names. [4] The identity of such characters, coming through costuming, grouping in relationship to major characters, and manner of participation in the narrative action of major characters, is exclusively in terms of social status (*a lord*), vocation (*a soldier*), dramatic function (*a messenger*), and relationship to a major character (*his servant*). In such instances, usually a name never appears in the dialogue; but, even when it does, its lack of prominence and frequency makes it an incidental feature of the conversation and situation of the stage personages rather than the means by which an audience identifies them. This incidental appellation should not influence critic, reader, or editor. For example, the stage-direction *Enter a Roman and a Volsce* in *Coriolanus* 4.3. accurately reflects the theatrical experience of a "mirror" or "choric" scene with two anonymous characters narratively unrelated to the events of the primary story — even though the names "Adrian" and "Nicanor" appear once each in the dialogue of the scene.

Even though we (probably) know the name "Angelica" for the Nurse in *Romeo,* its single, and late, appearance in the play (4.4) cannot influence the theatrical identification of her character. Instead, it is completely in terms of social status, vocation, dramatic type, and relationship to other characters: she is Juliet's nurse and a (comic) Capulet servant. Even though "Angelica" may appear as question or answer in some sophomore test (unfortunately, I think), it is totally independent of Shakespeare's dramaturgy. Editions which alter and supplement the rubrics of the folio and quartos are correct here in preserving *Juliet's Nurse* or *Nurse* throughout.

But editions in their stage-directions and speech-prefixes have frequently been misleading because they have preserved or added *names* which are not theatrically memorable and significant for minor characters comparable to the two choric figures in *Coriolanus* and for the unusual major characters like the Nurse in *Romeo.* Similarly, critics in their discussions have frequently been misleading because they have given prominence to an identification by name foreign to the theatre.

---

[4] Coghill presents an enlightening discussion of the significance of an exception —the prominent use of "Eros" in the dialogue of *Antony and Cleopatra*— in *Shakespeare's Professional Skills,* pp. 72-76.

Here I wish to make use of six plays —*Romeo, Coriolanus, Measure for Measure, Hamlet, Richard II,* and *The Merchant of Venice*— to illustrate the profit of exploring the theatrical context of Shakespeare's purposeful artistry in character identification.

The first act of *Measure for Measure* presents fifteen or sixteen characters, almost invariably identified in modern editions as Vincentio the Duke, Angelo, Escalus, Lucio, Mistress Overdone, Pompey, Claudio, the Provost, Juliet, Isabella —all appearing frequently in the play— and two gentlemen, officers, Friar Thomas, and Francisca a nun. But how would these various characters be identified by a theatre audience? That is, what appelative identifications are contained within the dramatic dialogue of the first act? Unquestionably, Angelo and Claudio are memorable names in the theatre: the dialogue contains sixty-one instances of "Angelo" and forty-three instances of "Claudio," including the prominence of anticipation, announcement, and direct-address. But the name "Vincentio" does not appear even once in the dialogue; the only knowledge of this name found in the folio comes in the list of "The names of all the Actors" at the conclusion of the text of the play. From costuming, he is immediately identified as a person of royal authority. As frequently noted in criticism of *Measure for Measure,* after the Duke has appointed Angelo his deputy during his absence, he stands above the action, overlooking and then manipulating it. The absence of a name for audience identification —the dependence upon the anonymity of social rank and vocation (royal authority) — strengthens the representational, even symbolic, nature of his function in the play. Shakespeare treats this Duke radically different from most major characters, including Angelo and Claudio in *Measure for Measure.* The play is not his story; his significance resides in *what* rather than uniquely *who* he is.

Narratively, this play identifies a number of minor characters by name. But the dialogue in the first act does *not* provide an instance of the names "Mistress Overdone," "Pompey," "Friar Thomas," or "Francisca." Thus, theatrically, these named characters do not exist. Rather, we have —using the terminology of the folio speech-prefixes— a *Bawd,* a *Clown,* a *Friar,* and a *Nun.* Dramatic significance of these four minor characters resides in social status, vocation, and association with conventionalized theatrical types. Probably all four would be immediately recognized by costuming.

Friar Thomas appears in only one scene, 1. 3. The audience, through dialogue, is given no means of identifying him as "Thomas." [5] And this emphasis on vocation rather than individuality is dramatically sufficient and even advantageous. The dramatic significance of 1. 3 resides in the Duke's comments on Angelo and in an awareness of his subsequent identity in disguise. It is not dependent upon an awareness of the uniqueness of the friar appearing with the Duke. This exclusively vocational identification accentuates the privacy of the Duke's remarks about testing Angelo. This scene creates no expectancy or apprehension that Angelo will learn of the Duke's testing and disguised presence, partly because the friar is anonymous, thus stressing his vocation, one associated with communication in confidence.

Francisca, a Nun, appears in only one scene, 1. 4. The dialogue omits any use of a name for her. Theatrically her identity is exclusively vocational, through costuming. Her dramatic function is as a nun, *any* nun: her presence immediately identifies her younger companion as Claudio's sister, for the earlier conversation between Claudio and Lucio had associated Isabella with a nunnery; the nun's presence with Isabella lends a credibility, a naturalism, to Lucio's entrance to Isabella. And the presence of a nun, any nun, with Isabella, together with their opening dialogue and the likelihood of Isabella's being garbed as a novice, increases an audience's awareness of Isabella's dilemma, the conflict between her religious convictions and her blood loyalties to Claudio.

Critical discussions using "Thomas" and "Francisca" and popular editions which reproduce the folio stage-directions containing these two names are employing a particularity foreign to Shakespeare's dramaturgy in these two scenes.

Particularly noteworthy in the examination of character identifications in *Measure for Measure* is, I think, the absence throughout the

[5] Such names for supernumeraries and minor characters are known from the stage-directions and speech-prefixes of the Folio, where the convenience of dramatic composition and theatrical production makes their presence understandable. Names of the characters in *Measure for Measure* are also found in "The names of all the Actors," the list in the Folio.

dialogue of the entire play of "Vincentio," the name usually associated with the Duke, a major character in the play. Examination of the entire text of *Coriolanus* produces similar and even more striking results: the names of four major characters in the play are mentioned infrequently and only incidentally in the dialogue. I speak of Junius Brutus, Sicinius Velutus, Volumnia, and Virgilia. Almost without exception, critics employ these four names foreign to Shakespeare's dramaturgy, surely purposeful dramaturgy because the absence of character names here contrasts sharply with his normal practice of appellative identification of major characters. Popular editions preserve these names from the Folio stage-directions and speech-prefixes, thus encouraging a reader to make untheatrical identifications.

Marcius first names the tribunes in 1.1.211-212:

> *Menenius.* What is granted them?
> *Marcius.* Five tribunes to defend their vulgar wisdoms,
> Of their own choice. One's Junius Brutus,
> Sicinius Velutus, and I know not — 'Sdeath!

But this reference is not in direct-address or an instance of the "look-where-he-comes" formula. The two tribunes have not appeared at this point. And this reference is not sufficiently prominent or obviously significant for an audience to remember it, for it to foreshadow the appearance of the tribunes, or for an audience to use it to identify the two by name at their subsequent first entrance. And the reference does not distinguish between the two tribunes. At their entrance together, the dialogue contains no instances of "Brutus" or "Sicinius." In their dialogue in this scene (1.1.247-274), the two tribunes do not use each other's name. Marcius' reference is, therefore, the only use of their names in the first scene in *Coriolanus*. From it an audience could not be expected to identify them by name.

The two tribunes are major characters, speaking much dialogue and frequently remaining on stage silent. They appear with much dialogue in 1.1, 2.1, 2.2, 3.1, 3.3, 4.2, 4.6, and 5.1. In each of these scenes the two enter and exit *together,* always functioning as a single political and dramatic force. Only in 5.4 does one appear on stage without the other. Neither addresses the other by name, and others address the two together as "Masters o' th' people" and "tribunes of the people," not by name. In only one passage other than Marcius' reference in 1.1 do their names appear:

> *All.* Tribunes! — Patricians! — Citizens! — What, ho!
> Sicinius! — Brutus! — Coriolanus! — Citizens!
> Peace, peace, peace! — Stay, hold, peace!
> *Menenius.* What is about to be? I am out of breath;
> Confusion's near; I cannot speak. You, tribunes
> To th' people! — Coriolanus, patience! —
> Speak, good Sicinius. (3.1.185-191)

But surely this single instance of direct-address, in a confusing stage situation, is too incidental and too late to assure that an audience will subsequently identify the tribunes as "Brutus" and "Sicinius." This absence of the names of the tribunes from the dialogue, with only the two less than forceful exceptions, can hardly be regarded as accidental or insignificant, for it varies so radically from Shakespeare's usual practices with major characters. That Shakespeare deliberately avoided the use of "Brutus" and "Sicinius" in the dialogue, particularly where it would have been memorable for an audience, seems an inescapable conclusion. And their consistent appearance together, similar to that of Rosencrantz and Guildenstern, Salarino and Salanio in *The Merchant of Venice,* and even Ross and Angus in *Macbeth,* works against the full individualization of either character. The two tribunes are, politically and theatrically, a single force throughout *Coriolanus.* Criticism should speak of only "the (two) tribunes," not of "Brutus" and "Sicinius." An edition which used *The Two Tribunes* in stage-directions and *First* and *Second Tribune* in speech-prefixes would be more faithful to the theatrical genre of the play than even the Folio.

The theatre audience's identification of Volumnia and Virgilia remains relational throughout the play —*Coriolanus' mother* and *wife.* "Virgilia" and "Volumnia" are found in the dialogue only once each— 1.3.120 and 5.4.55. But such incidental references cannot establish character identification. Again Shakespeare's treatment differs radically with his norm for major characters — prominent and frequent use of dialogue appellation. And again this unusual treatment is purposeful. For the dramatic function of these two women resides in their relationships to Coriolanus and their contrasting attitudes toward the military hero. *Mother* and *wife* —unnamed— accentuate the singularity of our concern in the play, Coriolanus. The narrative and historical names "Volumnia" and "Virgilia," found in North's Plutarch, have no proper place in criticism of Shakespeare's play — at least *as play*.

Romeo and Juliet 1.1 begins with the word-wit between two household servants. Most modern editions adhere to the opening stage-direction and speech-prefixes found in the quartos and Folio: *Enter Sampson and Gregory, of the house of Capulet, with swords and bucklers; Samson* and *Gregory*. The Elizabethan audience would probably assume that these two servants were only minor characters because of their social status. The entire play would bear out this judgment: neither servant appears in any subsequent scene. In 1.1 they are supernumeraries necessary to create the crescendo of conflict between Montagues and Capulets presented in the first seventy lines, conflict which is the troubled context of the love of hero and heroine. The opening wit from the two servants provides little information except that "Montagues" are their enemies, but its leisurely pace is vital to define the snowballing speed of the subsequent conflict between Tybalt and Benvolio, citizens, peace-officers, Old Capulet and Old Montague. Neither the dramatist nor the audience found individualization — identification by name— of such supernumeraries essential or even relevant. The dialogue twice (lines 1 and 70) mentions "Gregory" casually, but "Samson" is never used. The audience is, therefore, totally unaware of the name of one servant and only incidentally aware of the name of the other. [6] No dramatic cause, such as earlier foreshadowing or obvious social prominence, invests the two appellative references with any particular significance; no dramatic cause encourages the audience to remember the name "Gregory" in anticipation of this character's subsequent prominence in the action. Thus, the significance of these two characters resides entirely in terms of social status, vocation, and an incongruous detail — that the servants have weapons.

These two servants are of little consequence in the entire play, but Prince Escalus in his three vital interventions into the dramatic action is of considerable dramatic consequence. Yet the name "Escalus" is found only once in the substantive texts, in a stage-direction in 1.1. The name "Escalus" does not occur even once in the dialogue of the

---

[6] This appellative situation means, almost regretably, that the comic irony of Samson's cowardice is exclusively *literary*.

entire play, thus making it impossible for the theatre audience to identify him by name. Costuming identifies him as the Prince of the play. Even if his name "Escalus" were mentioned a dozen times, his dramatic significance would continue to reside essentially in *what* he is, not *who* in particular he is. He is the royal authority committed to the preservation of civil order, standing above the Capulet-Montague strife. The absence of his name enhances an audience's awareness of simply his social status (highest in the play) and vocation (royal authority representing peace and order). Shakespeare's treatment of him is thus parallel to that of the Duke in *Measure for Measure,* the unnamed Duke in *As You Like It,* and the unnamed King of France in *All's Well.*

Similarly, interpretations of *Hamlet* slightly dilute the sharpness of issues in the play by their prominent use of the name "Claudius" to identify the play's antagonist. For the dialogue of the play does not contain even one instance of this name. The antagonist is known from the dialogue to be Hamlet's uncle and, even more emphatically and continually, from costuming and stage-grouping to be *the king.* Because we as audience haven't seen the murder of Hamlet's father, haven't heard a soliloquy from Claudius admitting his villainy, or haven't been given some other proof of the ghost's truthfulness prior to his communication with Hamlet —that is, because our perspective, particularly through the play-within-a-play, is limited to Hamlet's perspective— we like Hamlet see *royal authority,* an apparent empirical contradiction to the charges leveled by the ghost. In the second scene, for example, we see a king respectfully surrounded by a court and vigorously dispatching private and public business. Our immediate visual experience is comparable to that of (anonymous) royal authority in other plays, such as the Prince in *Romeo.* The absence of the name "Claudius" from the dialogue, contrasting with Shakespeare's usual practice with major characters, is purposeful, just one additional facet of our awareness of the magnitude of the task given by the ghost. The duel of "mighty opposites" is between Hamlet and his uncle *the king.*

Shakespeare's history plays raise an additional problem about a theatre audience's character identifications: was the Elizabethan public-theatre audience sufficiently familiar with the historical situations dramatized to identify by name certain characters immediately, without

Shakespeare's usual means of individualized identifications? This complication excludes from my present discussion major characters in Shakespeare's English histories. But I believe that at least minor historical figures can be treated in the same manner as characters in the tragedies and comedies, that is, by looking within the text itself for evidence of visual and appellative identification. The Bishop of Carlisle in *Richard II* will illustrate. A minor character, he appears in just four scenes of the play: in 3.2 with King Richard, in 3.3 ("Flint Castle") with King Richard emblematically without one word of dialogue, in 4.1 ("deposition") with his long prophetic speech ("The blood of English shall manure the ground, / And future ages groan for this foul act"), and in 5.6, the play's final scene, to have his punishment administered by King Henry IV. His religious office would be visually evident upon each of these occasions through costuming. His name "Carlisle" appears only three times in the play, and two of these occasions —in the play's concluding scene— are too late to influence an audience's particularized identification of him. The first use of his name is hardly memorable: it is singular rather than repetitive; it is neither direct-address nor an instance of the "look-where-he-comes" formula since the Bishop is off-stage at the time; it is not preceded by any foreshadowing of the plot significance of this character.

> *Percy.* Yes, my good lord,
>   It doth contain a king. King Richard lies
>   Within the limits of yon lime and stone;
>   And with him are the Lord Aumerle, Lord Salisbury,
>   Sir Stephen Scroop, besides a clergyman
>   Of holy reverence; who, I cannot learn.
> *Northumberland.* O, belike it is the Bishop of Carlisle.
>
> (3.3.24-30)

In light of Shakespeare's repetitive and prominent use of names elsewhere, audience identification of the bishop in 3. 2, 3. 3, and 4. 1 is not part of his dramaturgy. But his generic identification as bishop through costuming is significant. Surely the function of Carlisle's prophetic speech in the deposition scene is "choric." And without the particularizing force of a memorable appellative identification, he represents the church; his words (and earlier his silent visual presence) possess the full authority of (anonymous) religious office. He is the play's *bishop* (unnamed in theatrical experience), thus strengthening the "choric" force of his words.

I suggest that instances such as Volumnia, Virgilia, Junius Brutus, and Sicinius Velutus from *Coriolanus*, Duke Vincentio, Prince Escalus, King Claudius, and the Bishop of Carlisle point up the significance of our looking at Shakespeare's stagecraft in matters of appellative or generic identification of characters as one additional evidence of Shakespeare's focus in a play — who is important, and as a *who* or a *what*. Certainly any full-fledged committment to Shakespeare's theatricality, to his artistry including "What the text makes the actor make the audience do," will include investigation of this small corner, Shakespeare's character identifications.

University of Georgia   CHARLES B. LOWER

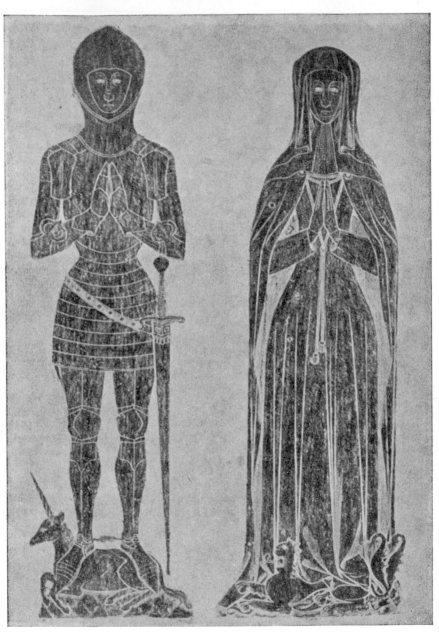

Thomas Chaucer and Wife (Ewelme, Oxfordshire)

The Mystery of Milton's Muse

THE OLD TRADITION that Milton's Muse is the Holy Ghost has been frequently questioned, [1] and the generally accepted view today seems most clearly expressed in Mr. Hanford's *Handbook* (New York, 1947, p. 194, n):

If one must have a theological formula it is best to say with Kelley that Milton's prayers are addressed to God the Father, and not to the Holy Spirit in any technical sense.

[1] Milton's third wife is reported in Newton's *Life of Milton* as saying that the Muse "was God's Grace and the Holy Spirit that visited him nightly," quoted by Todd *The Poetical Works of John Milton* [first ed. 1809] (London, 1852), III, 5, n. Todd himself unqualifiedly identifies the Muse of *Paradise Lost* and *Paradise Regained* as the Holy Ghost, (*ibid.,* I, 404-405, n). A. D. Barber, "The Religious Life and Opinions of John Milton," *Biblia Sacra*, XVII (1860), 28-34, and Arthur Sewell, *A Study of Milton's Christian Doctrine* (London, 1939), pp. 100-103, argue that Milton, by invoking the Holy Ghost in *Paradise Lost,* contradicted his prohibition in the *Christian Doctrine* against an invocation to the Holy Ghost (CE XIV, 394). Maurice Kelley, *This Great Argument* (Princeton, 1941), p. 111, disposes of this "contradiction" by concluding that Milton in *Paradise Lost* is invoking not the Holy Ghost, but "a personification of the various attributes of God the Father." My contention is that the *Christian Doctrine* prohibition of invocation applies in ecclesiastical and theological matters, that it repeats a Protestant commonplace enunciated dozens of times in *The Book of Common Prayer,* that the Holy Ghost in Milton's exegesis has no mediatorial functions, that Christ, the Son of God is "our only mediator and advocate," the "peerless lawyer" of Raleigh's "His Pilgrimage." *Nec invocandos* of the Latin theological treatise does not apply to literary invocations of *Paradise Lost* to a muse, who nevertheless may at times poetically be *Spiritus Sanctus.* A. W. Verity, 1895, in his notes to Book VII, appends an article, "Urania, the Heavenly Muse." He finds an indefiniteness as to the identity of the Muse, but believes that Milton "expressly distinguishes her from the Holy Spirit in Book I, 17-26." *Paradise Lost* (Cambridge, 1954), IV, 89. Gilbert Murray, *The Classical Tradition in Poetry* (Cambridge, Mass., 1927), p. 9, it may be inferred, anticipates part of the thesis of this article in his understanding of the first invocation, Book I, 17-19.

Recently, however, two scholars have identified the "Heav'nly Muse" as the Logos-Christ, [2] and Mr. Hughes seems inclined to agree with Tillyard that Milton's Muse is a "mystery that is inscrutable." [3] These, and other differing opinions as to the identity of Milton's Muse, leave the subject confused and undetermined.

This examination of the Muse presents the thesis that Milton's Muse is primarily a literary conceit which reflects prayers to the theological abstractions of the Father, the Son, *and* the Holy Ghost; that in making this multiple appeal, Milton is following the practice of Homer, Lucretius, Virgil, Dante, Tasso, Du Bartas, and Spenser. My point of view may be taken as an extension of B. Rajan's statement ". . . that Milton seems to go out of his way to avoid harassing the reader with his personal beliefs," or as a modified following through of an hypothesis that Maurice Kelley postulates: ". . . it may be that he never thought of his Muse in theological terms. . . ." [4] Milton's epic was thought by Dr. Johnson". . . to have been untouched by any heretical peculiarity of opinion." Joseph Addison states in his series of essays in *The Spectator* that Milton chose ". . . to confine himself to such thoughts as are drawn from the Books of the most Orthodox Divines, and to such Expressions as may be met with in Scripture." My contention is that divergent theologians may find in *Paradise Lost* confirmation of differing beliefs, that Trinitarian and anti-Trinitarian, Calvinist and Arminian may read *Paradise Lost* without offense or sense of contradiction. *Paradise Lost* is not a confession of faith, nor a creed; and Milton's invocations to the Heav'nly Muse are but il-

---

> . . . Thou, O Spirit, who dost prefer
> Before all temples the upright heart and pure
> Instruct me, for thou know'st, —

Murray says ". . . the prayer has passed imperceptibly from the throne of the Muse to that of the Holy Ghost."

Merrit Y. Hughes, "Milton and Light," *SEL*, IV (1965), 1-33, seems to agree with the statement of Kelley, p. 94, ". . . *Paradise Lost* III, 1-8 seems clearly an invocation to light in the physical sense." In *Complete Poems and Major Prose,* Mr. Hughes summarizes some ten conjectures as to the identity of Milton's Muse.

[2] Harry F. Robins, *If This Be Heresy* (Urbana, 1963), Chapter V, 157-175; William B. Hunter, Jr., "Milton's Urania," *SEL,* IV (1964), 35-41.

[3] *Complete Poems and Major Prose* (New York, 1957), p. 199. See also Kelley, p. 112, n. 74.

[4] *Paradise Lost and the Seventeenth-Century Reader* (London, 1962), p. 23; *This Great Argument,* p. 116.

lustrations and examples in microcosm of a neutral, perhaps scholarly, point of view that deliberately allows for varying interpretation or identification of the poet's sources of inspiration. This is not to say that there is conflicting belief between the unorthodox *De Doctrina Christiana* and an orthodox *Paradise Lost*. It is to say that the dogma of both pieces is presented on the basis of evidence available in the Bible and the literary-theological tradition of a divine epic. Milton's own personal belief is not heavily emphasized in either piece. *Paradise Lost* is the creation of a poet, a maker. *De Doctrina Christiana* is the work of an exegete, not a preacher or evangelist. Milton's Muse is an example of a union of eclectic concepts colored by Hebrew, Greek, and Christian tradition, a muse which reflects the light of all parts of a complicated and interrelated Trinity.

I

The tradition of the muse from Homer to Milton reveals a growth and an evolution. In the *Iliad* the muse is unnamed, but addressed variously as "goddess" (Θεά), "muse" (μουσα), or as "muses" (μουσαι). In the *Odessey* the invocation at the beginning of Book I is merely "O muse" (μοῦσα). [5] All muses are unnamed, bare and primitive by standards of Renaissance ornateness, or by standards of the *Homeric Hymns,* addressed to Apollo, Aphrodite, Pan, Artemis, and Calliope; or by standards of Pindar's Odes to Zeus, Olympia, Venus and the daughters of Cadmus.

Lucretius' *De Rerum Natura,* not really an epic, continues the practice of long serious poems of introducing materials by invocations, but to named muses, an address to Venus in Book I, 1-49, and to Calliope in Book VI, 93. [6] Seemingly dual invocations also appear in the *Aeneid.* In line 8 of Book I *a* muse is invoked, *O musa;* however,

[5] The invocations in the *Iliad* are in Book I, 1; II, 484-493, 761-762; XI, 218-220; XIV, 508-510; XVI, 112-113; in the *Odessy* I, 1. See William W. Minton, "Homer's Invocations of the Muses," *Transactions of the American Philological Association,* XC, (1960), 292-309.

[6] See Cyril Bailey, ed. *Lucretius: De Rerum Naturae* (Oxford, 1947), II, 589-591. See Pierre Boyance, *Le Culte des Muses Chez les Philosophes Grecs* (Paris, 1937).

with seeming unconcern for his commentators in Book VII, 37, Virgil invokes Erato. [7] Additionally in Book IX, 77, he invokes plural muses, *musae*. The prescription of Hesiod (*Theogony*, 73, 79) and Ovid (*Metamorphoses*, xxiv, 60) of Calliope as the muse of epic poetry seems disregarded. The actual practice of the poets generally does not seem to follow the identification of the mythological reference books.

Nor do the poets of the Renaissance confine themselves to one muse. Calliope is only one of many invoked, and her prominence in heroic verse itself is not above that of other muses. Dante has nine invocations in the *Divine Comedy*, one to Calliope. [8]

Tasso, among the heroic-divine poets who influenced Milton, seems to be the only one who confines himself to a single muse, and she is unnamed in the poem.

> O Musa, tu che dicaduchi allori
> Non cirondi la fronte in Elicona. ... [9]

Tasso, unless it is Milton himself, seems to be the only poet in the divine-heroic tradition who offers his prayer to only one muse.

Certainly Spenser in the proems to Book I and Book VI of *The Faerie Queene* invokes many, "Venus," Cupid, Elizabeth, "Virgin, Chief of Nyne," and "all ye impes that on Parnasso dwell." Additionally he invokes Clio by name in Book III, 3, 4. [10]

This multiplication of muses comes to a kind of finality in Sylvester's translation of Du Bartas' *Uranie* (1613). On the title page beside an imitation printed watermark, which encircles *Nove Musae Sylvestris*, are listed all nine muses. Despite his title-page listing of *all* the Greek

---

[7] See F. A. Todd, "Virgil's Invocation to Erato," *Classical Review*, XLV (1931), 216-218. Virgil invokes the muses a third time, Book IX, 77, "O Musae."

[8] Alighieri Dante, *La Divina Comedia*, ed. Sira A. Chimenza (Torino, 1963). See Irene Samuel, *Dante and Milton* (Ithaca, N. Y., 1966), p. 57.

[9] *La Gerusalemme Liberata*, ed. Fredi Chiappelli (Firenze, 1957), I, 2. Thomas Fairfax translated *Gerusalemme Liberata* into English in 1600. He renders *O Musa* as "Heavenly Muse," Milton's epithet. Sylvester uses the same phrase in his translation of Du Bartas' *Uranie*, 1613.

[10] D. T. Starnes, "Spenser and E. K.," *SP*, 49 (1944), 181-200; and D. T. Starnes and Ernest William Talbert, *Classical Myth and Legend in Renaissance Dictionaries* (Chapel Hill, 1955), 44-110, 226-339. Neither Spenser nor Milton follows only the limitations imposed upon the muses by dictionary definitions.

muses, in the poem Sylvester turns to diatribe against his earlier treatment of the pagan muses.

> You make chaste Clio, a light minion,
> Mount Helicon a stews. (Stanza 45)

> Employ no more the Elixir of your spirit
> Cytherea and her winged son. . . .
> But praise of David, Deborah, Judith. [11] (Stanza 59)

It seems that Du Bartas and Sylvester had lost faith in the classical muses, and had completely superseded them with the Christian muse Urania. It will be seen that Milton does not (*infra*). However, it is against her almost immediate literary background that Milton's Heav'nly Muse should be seen, and against the older pattern of multi-named muses, who seem to lose their identity, and with Du Bartas and Sylvester, their dignity and moral character. Todd, in his edition of Milton (1809) observes relative to Milton's first invocation (*P. L.*, I, 17): "Invoking the Muse is commonly a matter of mere form, wherein the poets neither mean, nor be thought to mean anything seriously." Cyril Bailey's edition of Lucretius' *De Rerum Natura* (II, 589) quotes Bayles' "Essay on Lucretius" as calling the invocation a *jeu d'esprit*.

II

The nature of Milton's Heav'nly Muse receives some amplification in the three main invocations in *Paradise Lost* (I, 1-26; III, 1-54; VII, 126), [12] and some suggestion of identity and number; but a careful

---

[11] *The Divine Weeks* (London, 1605). George C. Taylor, *Milton's Use of Du Bartas* (Cambridge, Mass., 1934) pp. 65-67, parallels Milton's invocations with similar expressions from *The Divine Weeks*. His thesis, I think completely proved, is that there are evident word echoes in Milton of Sylvester's translation. Mr. Taylor is not concerned with the device of the muse.

[12] A fourth invocation is frequently cited as appearing in Book IX, 1-48. However, since Milton there makes no request or prayer to his "Celestial Patroness," I prefer not to class it as an invocation, although it does, as almost all invocations do, summarize the following action of the poem. It has little bearing on the identity of the Muse or its relation to the Christian epic tradition.

analysis reveals *the* muse to be an indefinite, allusive concept, reflecting, however, three parts of the Trinitarian formulation of the Godhead, a rhetorical conceit with architectonic attributes which determine later treatments in the epic of his views of predestination, cosmology, and the "fortunate fall."

> Sing Heav'nly Muse, that on the secret top
> Of *Oreb* or of *Sinai*, didst inspire
> That Shepherd, who first taught the chosen Seed
> In the Beginning how the Heav'ns and Earth
> Rose out of *Chaos*: Or [italics mine] if *Sion* Hill
> Delight thee more, and *Siloa's* Brook that flow'd
> Fast by the Oracle of God; I thence
> Invoke thy aid to my advent'rous Song. ... (*P. L.*, I, 6-13)

If one takes the inspiration of "That Shepherd, [Moses as the author of *Genesis*] who first taught the chosen Seed / In the Beginning how the Heav'ns and Earth / Rose out of *Chaos*" as the inspiration of the Old Testament, he will find a parallel to the inspiration of the New Testament that comes from Sion Hill and Siloa's Brook that flowed past the Temple in Jerusalem. The inspiration of Moses, "before the Spirit was given," (*D. D. C.*, CE XIV, 359) in the Old Testament, would seem to be that of God the Father, and the inspiration of the New Testament might well be that of God the Son. However, a certain identification will not be possible in terms of the first paragraph in Chapter I of *De Doctrina Christiana*:

Under the name of Christ are comprehended Moses and the Prophets, who were his forerunners, and the Apostles whom he sent.

The reader who labors for a fine line of distinction here between the inspiration of the Old Testament and the New will not find it at the end of line 13 of the first invocation, although two sources of inspiration are clearly referred to; nevertheless they are separated with the word *or* (l. 10) and it would appear that either might be the source of inspiration invoked. The quotation immediately above from *De Doctrina Christiana* would indicate that the two are one.

The whole invocation, at this point, however, is only half complete. A third source, perhaps second to some readers, is prayed to:

And [italics mine] chiefly Thou O Spirit, that dost prefer
Before all Temples th'upright heart and pure,
Instruct me, for Thou knowst; Thou from the first
Wast present, and with mighty wings outspread
Dove-like satst brooding on the vast Abyss
And madst it pregnant: What in me is dark
Illumine, what is low raise and support. (*P. L.,* I, 18-24)

"Dove-like" is traditionally associated with the Holy Ghost (*Mark* 1. 10; *John* 1. 32) and "pregnant" reflects the Apostles' Creed phrase "conceived by the Holy Ghost," the Nicene Creed's reference to the Holy Ghost as "the Lord and Giver of Life." "And chiefly Thou O Spirit" then may appear as the third traditional part of the Trinity, as, indeed Mr. Hanford seems to have earlier thought: "The muse in Christian terminology is the Holy Ghost" (*Handbook,* New York, 1927, 149).

Thus, though there may be seen a Trinity in the identity of the Heav'nly Muse, its identity is not at all clearly a mathematical three-in-one, nor does Milton's language show anywhere an orthodox distinction between substance, subsistence, and essence; no three orders or co-equalities are implied. An Arian or Socinian would find only references to concepts in which he believed; similarly an orthodox Trinitarian would find no violation of his belief in Tri-unity. [13] Indeed, he might have seen in shifting references a triune fusion, as Dr. Johnson seems to have done.

III

Merrit Y. Hughes observes almost sadly "... if the invocation to Book III is our best key to Milton's art, we can only agree with Dr.

---

[13] Socinians and Arians did not deny the statements of the Apostles' Creed, which postulates a Father, a Son. and a Holy Ghost. See articles by William Fulton, "Trinity," and J. E. Carpenter, "Unitarianism," *HERE* (New York, 1919); J. H. Colligan, *The Arian Movement in England* (London, 1913), p. 5; *The Racovian Catechism* (London, 1656), p. 21: "The Quotations from the Bible only show that there is a Father, Sonne, and Holy Spirit to be three Persons in one Divine Essence"; J. P. Boyce, *Abstract of Systematic Theology* (Baltimore, 1932), pp. 74-75.

Tillyard that the mystery of his Muse is inscrutable." [14] Mr. Hughes himself seems to incline to a belief that "Holy Light" in the second invocation (*P. L.*, III, I-54) is God the Father or the Godhead as the source of Light. [15]

> Hail Holy Light, offspring of Heav'n first-born,
> *Or* [italics mine] of th' Eternal Coeternal beam
> May I express thee unblam'd? since God is Light,
> And never but in approached Light
> Dwelt from Eternity, dwelt then in thee,
> Bright effluence of bright essence increate.
> *Or* [italics mine] hear'st thou rather pure Ethereal stream,
> Whose Fountain who shall tell? (III, 1-8)

It is not difficult here, despite Mr. Robins' certainty to the contrary, [16] to identify "Heav'n first-born" with the Son of God of *De Doctrina Christiana*.

So also the Son is called the *first born*. ... the Son is said to be the *first born of every creature*, and *the beginning of the creation of God*. (CE XIV, 189)

Even if the phrase "offspring of Heav'n first-born" does identify the Son, the phrase does not exclusively confine itself to one identification. From *De Doctrina* the statement comes that the Spirit may be God himself, the Son of God, or "the Spirit of the Father and the Son" (CE XIV, 359-363). This multiplicity of identity and interrelated nature, it should be unnecessary to point out, is a well known commonplace of Christian theology, not what Milton unqualifiedly accepted as truth, but interpretations which had been set forth; and *De Doctrina* records them. This multiplicity and indefiniteness was the occasion of the controversies at Nicea in 325 and at Constantinople in 381, finally resolved in the Nicene Creed for the Western Church, which included the *filioque* clause specifying the double procession of the Spirit from the Father *and* the Son. Milton's invocation is to the "offspring of Heav'n first-born" *or* the offspring "of th' Eternal Coeternal beam." Reflected here seems clearly the *filioque* controversy of the early

---

[14] *Complete Poems and Major Prose*, p. 199.
[15] "Milton and Light," *SEL*, IV (1965), 31.
[16] *If This Be Heresy*, p. 166.

76

Church, a crux on which Milton is noncommittal in the poem, a crux which in *De Doctrina* he refers to as "so great a mystery" in his first paragraph "On the Holy Spirit" (CE XIV, 359). His next line in the poem, "May I express thee unblam'd?" seems to refer to the same controversy and to charges perhaps of heresy against those like Milton, who did not accept the formula of the double procession of the Spirit from the Father and the Son. [17] Milton's invocation will allow an appeal from either the Nicene or Greek creed, and, of course, from the Apostles' Creed, which does not refer to the procession of the Spirit.
A third appeal follows:

> *Or* [italics mine] hear'st thou rather pure Ethereal Stream
> Whose Fountain who shall tell? (III, 7-8)

It does not seem to be certain finally who is "Holy Light" or where she comes from. Milton's question is "who shall tell?" However, it is certain that whoever she is, or whatever it is, the concept invoked is a part of the Godhead.

> ... before the Sun,
> Before the Heavens thou wert, and at the voice
> Of God, as with a Mantle didst invest
> The rising world of waters dark and deep. (III, 9-11)

The *mysterious* implications of the Christian Godheard breed ambiguity and uncertainty, as is evident from Milton's third designation of the Spirit in *De Doctrina*.

Thirdly, the Spirit signifies a divine impulse, or light, or voice, or word, transmitted from above either through Christ, who is the Word of God, or by some other channel. (CE XIV, 367)

[17] "Unblamed" may be here a two-edged reference, *unblamed* by the orthodox, as suggested above, but also *unblamed* by the heterodox such as Milton was, or as his nephew Edward Phillips seems to have been, who in his dictionary, *The New World of Words* (London, 1678), defines the word *Trinitarian* as "a sort of heretics that deny the mystery of the Trinity." See William B. Hunter, Jr., "Some Problems of Miltonic Theological Vocablulary," *HTR*, LVII (1964) 364. "Milton might indeed believe that he was supporting the *homoousian* doctrine, the heart of the Nicene Creed."

This lack of final and exact identification is reflected again a few lines later in the poem when he assures us that he has not abandoned the old Greek muses, as Du Bartas and Sylvester had done.

> ... Yet not the more
> Cease I to wander where the Muses haunt
> Clear Spring, or Shady Grove, or Sunny Hill,
> Smit with the love of sacred Song. (III, 26-29)

Still more appealing than such traditionally pagan inspirations, however, is Christian inspiration,

> ... chief
> Thee *Sion,* and the flow'ry Brooks beneath
> That wash thy hallow'd feet. (III, 30-32)

"Thy hallowed feet" will not be appropriate to the Holy Ghost, God the Father, nor to "Holy Light." "Thy hallowed feet" are those of the Son or of the City of Jerusalem. If then "Holy Light" is God the Father, "offspring of Heav'n first-born" the Holy Ghost, and "hallowed feet" refer to God the Son, we have again allusion and implied invocation to all three persons of the Trinity.

A following of this intepretation of Milton's muse as tri-biguous or triune, without a unique identity of essence, will reveal the third invocation, Book VII, 1-12, as a restatement and a conclusion regarding his indeterminate but Christian muse.

> Descend from Heav'n *Urania,* by that name
> *If* [italics mine] rightly thou art call'd, whose Voice divine
> Following, above th'*Olympian* Hill I soar,
> Above the flight of *Pegasean* wing.
> The meaning, not the Name I call: for thou
> Nor of the Muses nine, nor on the top
> Of old *Olympus* dwell'st, but Heav'nlie borne,
> Before the Hills appear'd, or Fountain flow'd
> Thou with Eternal Wisdom [the *logos*] didst converse,
> Wisdom thy Sister, and with her didst play
> In presence of th'Almighty Father, pleas'd
> With thy Celestial Song.

Deliberately and with painstaking art, it would seem, then, that Milton has constructed a literary conceit, or literary "mystery," analo-

gous to a theological one, of which the Trinity is the foremost. Ter-
tullian is often quoted: *Credo quia impossible est* ("I believe because
it is impossible"). It is certain that Sir Thomas Browne was sincere
when he stated that a part of faith in a mystery was ". . . to believe a
thing not only above, but contrary to reason, and against the arguments
of the senses."[18]

Tillyard's characterization of Milton's Muse as "a mystery that is
inscrutable" may stand, and may have been intended by Milton to
stand for many readers; but the Muse would appear to be a deliberate
and contrived mystery, not inscrutable in terms of the usage of Homer,
Lucretius, Virgil, Dante, Tasso, or Spenser, in all of whom the muse
seems indefinite, multiple, many-named — somewhat mysterious. Nor
is the Muse "inscrutable" in a very literal sense of the word, in terms
of the complicated semantics of the Christian Trinity. The mystery of
Milton's Muse appears analogous to the *mystery* of the Trinity by
valid and factual coincidence, and analagous by deliberate and
conscious intent of the poet.

With Milton the prayer of invocation is, as Hanford and Kelley
have long contended, to the Godhead; but since many names ("not"
the "meaning") are involved in the Judaeo-Christian Godhead, Milton
by allusion and almost imperceptible shifting of reference seems to in-
voke as many as seem appropriate to all Christian readers. But Robins
and Hunter certainly have justification for their contention that the
Muse is the Logos-Christ. The contention of this paper is that parts
of the invocations are certainly to the Logos-Son; and the old
identification of the Muse as the Holy Ghost has very solid evidence
to support its validity in parts of the invocations.

The Muse is named Urania, Heav'nly Muse, O Spirit, Holy Light,
Offspring of Heav'n first-born, Celestial Patroness; but Milton's

[18] *Religio Medici*, ed. Bohn. (London, 1910), II, 20. The possibility for
divergent views on the orthodox formulation of the Trinity is great.
    The orthodox Trinity presents within one eternal essence three co-essential,
tri-personal divine co-equal subsistencies, who are ranked in three orders. The
enormous complications of the whole Trinitarian controversy are detailed at
length in J. N. D. Kelly's *Early Christian Doctrine* (London, 1958), pp. 83-348.
The development of the Trinitarian tradition up to the end of the nineteenth
century is summarized with clarity by George Park Fisher, *History of Christian
Dogma* (Edinburgh, 1896). See also Ruth Montgomery Kivette, *Milton on the
Trinity* (Ann Arbor: University Microfilms, 1960).

semantic clarity, not always evident, probably deliberately obscured in these invocations, seems wholly clear in the invocation to Book VII: "The meaning, not the name I call." This same semantic intent, with conjunctive and disjunctive qualification, seems evident in the invocations of Books I and III. The "Heav'nly Muse" of Book I dwelt on Horeb *or* Sinai, *or* Sion Hill; "*And* Chiefly Thou, O Spirit" seems to make the object of invocation multiple. "Holy Light" in Book III is "offspring of Heav'n first-born" *or* "of the eternal coeternal beam." [19] The overall plea is made to the Christian Godhead: whether to God the Father, God the Son, or to God the Holy Ghost seems relatively unimportant; all parts are reflected, and neither Trinitarian nor anti-Trinitarian will find sure evidence to disabuse him of a conviction that Urania is a Christian muse reflecting three parts of the Godhead.

IV

Some of Milton's and/or attitude of conjunction and disjunction in his treatment of the exact identity of the Muse carries over into the presentation of soteriology and cosmology in *Paradise Lost*.

A decision, for instance, as to whether the poem presents an Arminian concept of Predestination should not be an absolute one. In Book III, 55-166, the Son has seen Satan, escaped from Hell, flying toward the earth. He asks the Father if man, "thy youngest son," shall "Fall circumvented thus by fraud. ..." The Father's answer is undoubtedly primarily the Arminian one. [20]

> ... I made him just and right,
> Sufficient to have stood, though free to fall. (III, 98-99)

> ... they themselves decreed
> Their own revolt, not I. (III, 116-117)

---

[19] My position appears in disagreement with that of Maurice Kelley (p. 92) and Hughes ("Milton and Light," p. 31). "The pure ethereal stream" seems in this context to be part of the Godhead, not, as they contend, light in the physical sense.

[20] Kelley, pp. 82-84.

Yet at the conclusion in the poem of this Arminian explanation of salvation the Father tells the Son:

> Some I have chosen of peculiar grace
> Elect above the rest; so is my will. (III, 183-184)

"Elect above the rest" reflects a concept agreeable to the Calvinist reader of the poem, [21] as do the lines having to do with grace, "As my Eternal purpose hath decreed":

> Man shall not quite be lost, but sav'd who will,
> Yet not of will in him, but grace in me
> Freely voutsaf't. (III, 172-175)

Without the Latin *De Doctrina* before him and a copius fund of theology in a precise understanding, the seventeenth and eighteenth century reader would have been hard put to discover in *Paradise Lost* conclusive evidence to discredit the Calvanistic scheme of Predestination and election. In our own time, however, Maurice Kelley has shown rather conclusively that these lines accurately interpreted are an expression of the Arminian plan allowing a free will to man, which the Calvinist denied him. [22]

The reader of the whole of *Paradise Lost* remembers well the Ptolemaic cosmology of the poem and probably also Raphael's question as to whether or not the Copernican system be a true explanation of the system around the earth: "What if the Sun be the center of the World?" (VIII, 122-158). Man's inability to comprehend the real truth about the whole starry creation is clear in Raphael's admonition to Adam.

> Solicit not thy thoughts with matters hid
> ... Heav'n is for thee too high. (VIII, 167, 172)

Neither Raphael nor Milton seems to have a preference as to the truth of either system.

[21] Nat. V. Daniel, "The Theology of *Paradise Lost* III, 183-184 Reexamined," *RenP, 1963,* pp. 21-29, expressing a view not dissimilar to that of this paper, says Milton "... compressed everything the Bible says about any kind of election into the lines 183-184 without defining its terms, and therefore without interpretation in any way."

[22] Kelley, p. 15.

The whole explanation by the "Divine Instructor," Raphael, had begun back in Book V with the caveat that comprehension of the battle in heaven and knowledge about the constitution of the Cosmos involves secret knowledge, "Not lawful to reveal."

> ... yet for thy good
> This is dispensed, and what surmounts the reach
> Of Human sense, I shall delineate so,

> ... though what if Earth
> Be but the Shadow of Heav'n, and things therein
> Each to other like, more than on Earth is thought? (V, 5705-76)

Neither the followers of Ptolemy, who were vocal in the seventeenth century,[23] nor the Copernican astronomers seem to have registered exception to these two noncommittal accounts. In the poem the two systems are the two preferred seventeenth-century explanations. The reader is neither urged nor persuaded to accept either. The implication is that Man never will understand the Cosmos.

And finally, what is usually conceived as the sad main theme of the whole poem, "Of Man's disobedience and the fruit of that forbidden tree," Adam views as a fortuitous happening, the "fortunate fall," which, as we know, is the old *felix culpa* of Christian tradition going back certainly as far as Augustine.[24] Michael in the last two books has shown Adam the history of the world as it is related in the Old and New Testaments and has explained how the Son of God and Man will redeem Mankind. Even after Adam has been informed of his sentence of death and his sentence to work by the sweat of his brow, he is exultant.

> O Prophet of glad tidings, finisher
> Of utmost hope! (XII, 375-376)

> O goodness infinite, goodness immense!
> That all this good of evil shall produce,

[23] See David Masson, *Life of Milton* (London, 1861), II, 121. "In 1640 the Copernican theory seems universally accepted as a delusion."
[24] Arthur O. Lovejoy, "Milton and the Paradox of the Fortunate Fall," *ELH*, IV (1937), 161-179.

And evil turn to good; more wonderful
Than that which by creation first brought forth
Light out of darkness! full of doubt I stand
Whether I should repent me now of sin
By me done and occasiond, or rejoice. (XII, 469-475)

"... full of doubt" as to whether he should repent or *rejoice* that he had sinned? Milton does not commit Adam, Michael, or himself. The "fit audience though few" are left with this problem of Christian soteriology to view as they see fit.

If the drama here is main and central to the whole epic, if the "fortunate fall" forms an emphatic organic feature of the whole poem, Douglas Bush's assertion that there is "no central antinomy" in *Paradise Lost* [25] is open to question. In conclusion — I do not think Robert Adams in 1955 was referring to the elements of the poem reflecting Milton's Muse, cosmology, or soteriology. Nevertheless, his remarks referring to Milton's noncommittal treatments of evil attitudes in the speeches of Satan and his followers, may well serve as a summary for this paper. "The antinomy on which Milton's work centers undergoes full exploration, not a full solution." [26]

University of Richmond   NATHANIEL H. HENRY

[25] Douglas Bush, *Paradise Lost in Our Time* (Ithaca, N. Y., 1945), p. 205, n.
[26] Robert Adams, *Ikon: John Milton and the Modern Critics* (Ithaca, N. Y., 1955), p. 207.

Margaret Cheyne (Hever, Kent)

Point of View in *Paradise Lost:* Books I-IV

MILTON'S MANIPULATION of point of view in *Paradise Lost,* begins early in Book I with the rhetorical question, "Say first what cause/ Mov'd our Grand Parents in that happy State,/ Favor'd of Heav'n so highly, to fall off/ . . .Who first seduc'd them to that foul revolt?" (I, 28-33).* The answer involves a transition to the environs of Hell, where the action begins by focusing on Satan:

> Th' infernal Serpent; hee it was. . .
> . . . Him the Almighty Power
> Hurl'd headlong flaming from th' Ethereal Sky
> With hideous ruin and combustion down
> To bottomless perdition, there to dwell
> In Adamantine Chains and penal Fire. (I, 34-48)

These lines signal a change in point of view, from the Narrator's opening statement and invocation to Satan reviving on the burning lake. From this point until the end of Book II the action is presented from a carefully limited point of view. It is the view from Hell. As the poem begins we see only Hell and its inhabitants. God and the other major personae of the poem are seen most powerfully through the distorted vision of Satan and his followers. The cosmos beyond is at this point indefinite, except as we get brief hints of it through the account of the fall by Satan, Beëlzebub, and others, and as we hear the generalized comments of the Narrator, insisting upon a broader and contradictory vision. Even the Narrator, however, seems to be speaking from Hell, and primarily in reaction to Satan.

---

* All quotations from *Paradise Lost* are taken from Merritt Y. Hughes, *John Milton: Complete Poems and Major Prose* (New York, 1957).

85

Milton, then, has presented us with a distorted vision at the beginning of the poem. We might allude to the old formula of beginning *in medias res* to account for the poem's opening. But this is, at best, a superficial answer. The action not only begins in Hell; it is *seen* from Hell. And the restricted point of view is fundamental in producing the initial, emphatic distortion which has produced so much critical confusion. This perspective gives Satan more prominence than he would otherwise have, and, read out of context, has caused many critics to see Satan as the hero of the poem, as the character with whom Milton could most sympathetically, although perhaps unconsciously, identify. Such an interpretation tends to depreciate Milton's artistry, portraying him as succeeding almost despite his conscious intentions. An examination of Books I and II in the context of the whole poem, or even of the first four books, will reveal, however, a narrative technique at work rather than an unconscious identification. There is, simply in terms of narrative effectiveness, a reason for the dominance of Satan in the opening books. Milton was faced with an extremely difficult problem: he must establish Satan as a serious adversary and at the same time assert God's omnipotence. How was he to maintain God's omnipotence without destroying all semblance of conflict and tension in the poem? The answer lies, I believe, primarily in his use of point of view.

From the limited perspective of Hell Satan can seem to be a formidable adversary. The speeches, the actions, and most of the descriptive passages emphasize the "heroic" defiance and the power of the "Arch-Angel ruin'd," and since at this point we have no other *dramatized* character for comparison only the voice of the Narrator, which later through its persistent interpretative commentary and through its dramatization in the recurrent invocations becomes a kind of persona in its own right, but which at this point seems abstract and clearly outside of the action — we are forced, willingly or not, to take Satan and his followers at their own valuation, or at least to judge them primarily in terms of what they tell us about themselves.

The picture that we get is one of unswerving malevolence which has matched arms with the Almighty and just barely failed of success. Satan says,

> All is not lost; the unconquerable Will,
> And study of revenge, immortal hate,

86

> And courage never to submit or yield:
> And what is else not to be overcome?
> That Glory never shall his wrath or might
> Extort from me. To bow and sue for grace
> With suppliant knee, and deify his power
> Who from the terror of this Arm so late
> Doubted his Empire, that were low indeed,
> That were an ignominy and shame beneath
> This downfall.   (I, 106-116)

And further,

> To do aught good never will be our task,
> But ever to do ill our sole delight,
> As being the contrary to his high will
> Whom we resist. If then his Providence
> Out of our evil seek to bring forth good,
> Our labor must be to pervert that end,
> And out of good still to find means of evil;
> Which oft-times may succeed, so as perhaps
> Shall grieve him, if I fail not, and disturb
> His inmost counsels from their destin'd aim. (I, 159-168)

The Satanic malevolence is vividly established, and lacking God's perspective, we are prone to interpret the partial victories to which Satan aspires, and which we know he will gain, from his own viewpoint. There is, of course, as has been pointed out by Waldock, Anne Ferry, and others, a persistent counterpoint to this point of view in the voice of the Narrator. We are, in a sense, being given a double vision. For instance, after Satan's opening speech of defiance, the Narrator comments,

> So spake th' Apostate Angel, though in pain,
> Vaunting aloud, but rackt with deep despair. (I, 125-126)

And after Satan's next speech, he remarks,

> So stretcht out huge in length the Arch-fiend lay
> Chain'd on the burning Lake, nor ever thence
> Had ris'n or heav'd his head, but that the will
> And high permission of all-ruling Heaven
> Left him at large to his own dark designs. (I, 209-213)

Waldock quite rightly points out the antithetical nature of the speeches of Satan and the comments of the Narrator, and he also stresses the greater impact of Satan's dramatic speeches as opposed to the mere allegations of the Narrator.

Waldock says,

> If one observes what is happening one sees that there is hardly a great speech of Satan's that Milton is not at pains to correct, to damp down and neutralize. He will put some glorious thing in Satan's mouth, then, anxious about the effect of it, will pull us gently by the sleeve, saying (for this is what it amounts to): 'Do not be carried away by this fellow: he *sounds* splendid, but take my word for it ...' We have in fact ... two levels: the level of demonstration or exhibition, and the level of allegation or commentary; and ... there is disagreement. What is conveyed on one level is for a large part of the time not in accord with what is conveyed on the other. Milton's allegations *clash* with his demonstrations.
>
> (A. J. A. Waldock, *Paradise Lost and Its Critics*, pp. 77-78)

These remarks are based on the facts of the poem and except for the connotations of their accusatory tone are, I believe, right. But his next generalization I find emphatically wrong. "Each great speech," Waldock says, "lifts Satan a little beyond what Milton really intended, so he suppresses him again (or tries to) in a comment" (*ibid.*, pp. 78-79). Waldock's conceptions of narrative excellence seem to blind him to other narrative possibilities. He says with finality, "In any work of literature at all it is the demonstration, by the very nature of the case, that has the higher validity: an allegation can possess no comparable authority" (*ibid.*, p. 78). But perhaps what looks like a blemish in a limited passage may in a broader perspective come to be seen as a justifiable narrative device.

Satan has not gotten out of hand; rather he has been deliberately heightened, primarily through the use of a highly selective point of view. In the first two books we are given a limited (and therefore distorted) perspective so that Satan can seem to be a convincing adversary of God. And this is necessary for the success of the poem. Unless the challenge to God's omnipotence is strong enough to raise at least momentary doubts, there can be no serious conflict in the poem.

88

Yet, given Milton's purpose, the doubt must be a temporary one. Hence the Narrator's commentary, which is not an attempt to compensate for a momentary loss of control, but rather a proleptic device. It is not intended to negate the perspective from Hell, but to prepare us for a more inclusive vision which will succeed it. For the moment, however, it is subordinated to Satan's rhetoric. Through the distortion of this limited perspective, Satan is presented as a convincing threat to Adam and Eve and as a serious opponent to the Almighty.

There is, then, in the first two books of *Paradise Lost* a tension between an abstract omniscient voice which constantly suggests a broader perspective without fully revealing it and a cast of dramatized characters who see the action only from their own limited perspectives within the confines of Hell. The point of view of the first two books is a composite of these two conflicting perspectives. The limited perspective of Satan and his followers dominates the reader's initial impressions, while the voice of the narrator, with its persistent counterpoint, prepares him for the broadening perspective which begins with the view from Heaven in Book III.

Before the drastic shift of perspective in Book III, however, there is a gradual modification of Satan's character. In the first two books a threat is established and then gradually focused on Paradise, but by the time the target has been selected the threat has changed from one of overwhelming physical violence (represented by the armed masses of Satan's legions) to one of subtle deceit and seduction. This new emphasis is first seen in the perverse rhetoric of Satan's speeches and in his manipulation of the debate in Book II, and is continued in his encounters with Sin, Death, and Chaos, where he shrewdly appraises the nature of his opponents and adjusts his approach to fit the bias of each.

The first major disruption of the Satan-centered perspective comes at the beginning of Book III. The limited view from Hell is suddenly replaced by a total perspective, as God, surrounded by Christ and the unfallen angels, looks down on the cosmos and its inhabitants from Heaven.

> Now had th' Almighty Father from above,
> From the pure Empyrean where he sits

High thron'd above all highth, bent down his eye,
His own works and their works at once to view:
About him all the Sanctities of Heaven
Stood thick as Stars, and from his sight receiv'd
Beatitude past utterance; on his right
The radiant image of his Glory sat,
His only Son; On Earth he first beheld
Our two first Parents, yet the only two
Of mankind, in the happy Garden plac't,
Reaping immortal fruits of joy and love,
Uninterrupted joy, unrivall'd love
In blissful solitude. He then survey'd
Hell and the Gulf between, and *Satan* there
Coasting the wall of Heav'n on this side Night
In the dun Air sublime, and ready now
To stoop with wearied wings, and willing feet
On the bare outside of this World. (III, 56-74)

For the first time in the poem all of the characters are seen at once. The perspective, as seen through the eyes of God is total, although the participants below continue to see the situation only from their own limited points of view. The action stops while God makes an interpretative commentary on the action of the whole poem, looking backward and forward from the point where the action below has lapsed.

Many critics have commented on the strategic error of Milton's presenting God as a character pronouncing the theological rationale of the poem. In one sense they are right. God simply is not a successful character here. This is, dramatically, one of the least effective scenes in the poem. Nevertheless, it is vital to the success of the poem. Satan, having dominated the first two books, must, given Milton's purpose, be placed in his proper perspective or he *will* become the hero of *Paradise Lost*. Generally, in fact, the reader must be reminded of what in broad outline he already knows in order to keep him from becoming disoriented by a partial perspective, whether it be Adam's, Eve's, or Satan's. God becomes a vehicle for this overview. Technically, he becomes a point of view, the total view, overriding the partial view which has dominated the reader's perceptions up to this point. Increasingly (until Satan's metamorphosis in Book X at least) we become aware of the validity of the asides which the narrator had interjected in Books I and II. From this point on, the action of the epic rather than conflicting with the voice of the narrator reinforces it.

90

The initial impression of Books I and II lingers on, however, even after the shock of seeing Satan through God's eyes — perhaps because God's view was a commentary outside the action proper and not yet dramatically realized. But we get yet another shock in Book IV, when Satan himself reveals in his first soliloquy the falseness of our earlier impressions.

> Me miserable! which way shall I fly
> Infinite wrath and infinite despair?
> Which way I fly is Hell; myself am Hell;
> And in the lowest deep a lower deep
> Still threat'ning to devour me opens wide,
> To which the Hell I suffer seems a Heav'n.
> O then at last relent: is there no place
> Left for Repentance, none for Pardon left?
> None left but by submission; and that word
> *Disdain* forbids me, and my dread of shame
> Among the Spirits beneath, whom I seduc'd
> With other promises and other vaunts
> Than to submit, boasting I could subdue
> Th' Omnipotent. Ay me, they little know
> How dearly I abide that boast so vain,
> Under what torments inwardly I groan:
> While they adore me on the Throne of Hell,
> With Diadem and Sceptre high advanc'd
> The lower still I fall, only Supreme
> In misery; such joy Ambition finds. (IV, 73-92)

This weakness is momentary, of course, and he ends the speech confirmed in evil,

> Farewell Remorse; all Good to me is lost;
> Evil be thou my Good (IV, 109-110)

But we cannot again view him in the same way that we did in Book I. In fact, in retrospect, what seemed to be heroic defiance in Book I,

> The mind is its own place, and in itself
> Can make a Heav'n of Hell, a Hell of Heav'n.
> What matter where, if I be still the same, (I, 254-256)

now can only be seen ironically.

91

Gradually as the poem develops, we see Satan in different contexts and from different perspectives, and our initial impressions are modified. This gradual revelation is produced both by his own soliloquies, which in their hesitations and doubts render him more commensurate with his mere human opponents, and by a series of encounters, first with his allies (Sin, Death, Chaos), then with Uriel, and finally, at the end of Book IV, with Gabriel and the angelic watch. These encounters establish a minor pattern of their own. In the early encounters (with Sin and Death, Chaos, and Uriel) he performs so flawlessly as spy and flatterer that we begin to see him as a different kind of threat from the military leader of Book I. Without his armed host and in situations that demand guile rather than the large public gesture, he emerges as a master of deceit. But just as we are becoming confident of his continued success, he suffers a setback in his encounter with Gabriel and the watch. Once his menace as a deceiver has been established, it is qualified in order to preserve a degree of suspense. If he is clever enough to deceive even the archangel Uriel, surely he poses a threat to the inexperienced Adam and Eve. Yet he has been withstood by Ithuriel and Zephon, and scornfully exposed by Gabriel.

These encounters create a fine ambivalence presided over and heightened by the appearance in the heavens of the scales, symbolic of God's omnipotence. Satan flees. By this time we are sufficiently aware of Satan's role in the total context of the poem. The stage has been set for the temptation. Now the emphasis can shift to Adam and Eve.

Adam and Eve, incidentally, like Satan, function as limited points of view. They, too, are essential to the method of gradual revelation which controls the narrative progression of the poem. We see more than they do, but we also see *as* they do. In other words, dramatic irony and a gradually widening focus are essential features of Milton's method of presentation. Our awareness of the total pattern of meaning expands, like Adam's from a limited, imperfect perception toward a gradual, full comprehension. The pattern of an initial limited view which is gradually expanded is enacted in miniature in the first four books of *Paradise Lost,* but it continues throughout the poem, and it is completed only in the final book.

University of North Carolina   WILLIAM A. McQUEEN

Sexual Metaphor in Milton's Cosmogony, Physics, and Ontology

W. B. C. WATKINS has written that in *Paradise Lost* Milton relegated sexual imagery to the surrounding universe in order to express God's generative abundance. [1] This is to say that the male-female principle, skillfully symbolized in the relationship between Adam and Eve, is one of the controlling ideas of the poem and that its extension into the cosmos authenticates and subtilizes the erotic motives in Milton's epic. The symbolism works in two directions: images of human fertility move outward into the universe; and images of cosmic fertility, in turn, look toward man as the symbol of divine generation. Thus, ordinary masculine and feminine roles join symbolically in the procreative effluence of God. A reflex, in consequence, exists between mundane and supermundane sexuality. The principle of correspondence applies as Raphael states the philosophical basis of Milton's symbolism:

> ... how last unfold
> The secrets of another World, perhaps
> Not lawful to reveal? yet for thy good
> This is dispens't, and what surmounts the reach
> Of human sense, I shall delineate so,
> By lik'ning spiritual to corporal forms,
> As may express them best, though what if Earth
> Be but the shadow of Heav'n, and things therein
> Each to other like, more than on Earth is thought? [2]

---

[1] *An Anatomy of Milton's Verse* (Baton Rouge, La., 1955), p. 62. See pp. 42-83, 126-146. Joseph Summers also writes: "The theme of the 'two great Sexes' is central to the entire poem. A recognition of its role provides one of the most immediately accessible ways into the meaning and method of *Paradise Lost*" (*The Muse's Method*, Cambridge, 1962, p. 109).

[2] *Paradise Lost*, V, 568-576. This and all subsequence references, which will be given in the text, are to Merritt Y. Hughes' edition of Milton's *Complete Poems and Major Prose* (New York, 1957).

On this authority Milton externalizes images of human sexuality into the cosmos and transforms the physics of the universe into poetic utterance.

Milton repeatedly associates Adam with the sun and Eve with both the moon and the earth. These identifications are thoroughly grounded in Platonic philosophy, though any number of individual sources could be adduced to support what was by the time of the Renaissance a literary commonplace. [3] The Eve-moon/Adam-sun parallelism was obviously pat to Milton's purpose of showing female subordination to male authority and of making the harmony of the heavens a paradigm of human order. Illustrative are Raphael's words to Adam telescoping cosmogonic and human sexuality:

> ... and other Suns perhaps
> With thir attendant Moons thou wilt descry
> Communicating Male and Female Light,
> Which two great Sexes animate the World. (VIII, 148-151)

Raphael's account of the formation of the celestial bodies describes the relationship between Adam and Eve exactly: as Eve followed Adam in the order of creation, so God created the sun first and then the moon (VII, 354-357). Again Raphael's words, descriptive of the heavenly bodies, are apposite to Adam and Eve:

> ... less bright the Moon,
> But opposite in levell'd West was set
> His mirror, with full face borrowing her Light
> From him, for other light she needed none. (VII, 375-378)

Working within the enveloping imagery of sun and moon, two other images in this passage (the mirror and light) mediate the analogous

---

[3] Plato's Ideas and Space are a function of the male-female principle at the cosmic level and thus constitute the philosophical basis for the traditional correspondence of female-earth and male-sun. Feminine Space is "the mother and receptacle" of masculine Ideas (*Timaeus,* 51A). Proclus, in turn, says that all divinities proceed analogous to Heaven and Earth, with Heaven having the relation of father and Earth of mother (*The Six Books of Proclus,* trans. Thomas Taylor, London, 1816, II, 193-194). Ficino brings the idea into the Renaissance by fusing the archetypal symbol of light into his philosophy of love, endowing the heavenly bodies and his ethical vision with sexuality, and identifying a parallelism between them all (*Commentary on Plato's "Symposium,"* trans. Sears Jayne, Columbia, Missouri, 1944, pp. 156 ff.).

relationship between male and female. Both evoke traditional philosophical and literary meanings, the more so in *Paradise Lost* because of the mirror-reflection configuration that dominates much of the poem. [4] As Eve contemplates her own perfection in a pool of water, so Adam sees himself reflected in Eve. Light is the traditional symbol for the creative power emanating from God. In this context, Eve's fertility subsists in the generative potency of Adam; and "With borrow'd light her countenance triform / Hence fills and empties to enlighten the Earth" (III, 730-731). The science of the universe is thus the biology of human life: impregnated wombs grow and issue in the continuing promise of life.

Once one has recognized that human sexuality is the hieroglyph of divine fertility, he understands how Milton humanizes the universe and at the same time spiritualizes the first facts of life. Milton's account of creation gains thereby because it corresponds organically with human generation and because it is a cosmic enactment of man's dependence on God. In the person of Christ, God *said* and

> ... the Earth obey'd, and straight
> Op'ning her fertile Womb teem'd at a Birth
> Innumerous living Creatures, perfect forms,
> Limb'd and full grown: out of the ground up rose. (VII, 453-456)

Christ, then, through a process of symbolic linking, is both the sun and light. Through these natural agencies he calls forth the creatures of the world. Just as man has his being in God, so the moon has its being in the reflected light of the sun. So also Eve has hers in Adam. The symbolic equivalence is such that Christ, the sun, light, and Adam (a masculine configuration) are interchangeable ciphers in a divine equation that balances a feminine configuration made up of the earth, moon, and Eve, which two image clusters combine in turn to yield Milton's monistic God.

This kind of symbolic linking, which Milton could have learned from Neoplatonic mythologies, enables the poet to fuse many levels of meaning —ontological, cosmological, psychological, and ethical— into a dynamic whole:

---

[4] See Cleanth Brooks, "Eve's Awakening," in *Essays in Honor of Walter Clyde Curry* (Nashville, Tenn., 1954).

... The Earth
Though, in comparison of Heav'n, so small,
Nor glistering, may of solid good contain
More plenty than the Sun that barren shines,
Whose virtue on itself works no effect,
But in the fruitful Earth; there first receiv'd
His beams, unactive else, thir vigor find. (VIII, 91-97)

It is obvious here that Milton conceives the Earth as matter, the female principle of the universe, and the Sun as form, the male principle. Milton probably learned the doctrine from Aristotle, who asserted with a lucidity that Plato might well have envied that "the male and female principles may be put down first and foremost as origins of generation, the former as containing the efficient cause of generation, the latter the material of it." [5] In Milton's treatment, following Aristotle, each principle is necessary to the other if either is to be fruitful. Nature's law is such that all causes act according "to the reception of thir matter" and "not to th' extent of thir own Sphere" (X, 805-808). Newton explained *reception* by quoting the axiom: "Every efficient (i. e., everything which acts) acts according to the powers of what receives its action, not according to its own powers." [6] Aristotle expressed the same idea when he said that potentiality existed in matter and not in form. Put another way, that which creates is limited by that on which and in which it works. Applying this principle to human generation both physical and spiritual, Eve as the receiving principle limits the efficient powers of Adam. As such she is not only his "other self" but the very boundaries of his existence. In another context, she is the Moon, a "moist Continent" exhaling "nourishment" to "higher Orbs": "The Sun that light imparts to all, receives /From all his alimental recompense" (V, 423-424). [7] The physics of the Heavens is such, therefore, that the mechanical becomes organic. Thus, the Sun's "fervid Rays" warm "Earth's inmost womb" (V, 301-302) to bring forth new forms of life, while the stars prepare the Earth "to receive / Perfection from the Sun's more potent Ray" (IV, 673).

[5] *De generatione animalium,* trans. Arthur Platt, in *The Works of Aristotle* (Oxford, 1912), V, 716a5.
[6] Quoted in Hughes, pp. 425-426, n. 807.
[7] Hughes (p. 312, n. 415-426) elaborates this doctrine by citing Plato's *Timaeus,* Lipsius' *Physiologiae Stoicorum,* and (among others) Pliny's *Natural History.*

Along with Sin and Death, Chaos and Old Night are the chief allegorical representations in *Paradise Lost*. Significantly, Chaos is a male figure and Night his female consort. His throne borders on light,

> ... and his dark Pavilion spread
> Wide on the wasteful Deep; with him Enthron'd
> Sat Sable-vested *Night*, eldest of things,
> The Consort of his Reign. (II, 960-963)

Milton consistently identifies Night and Chaos with the womb of nature, with uncreated matter, with the "unreal, vast, unbounded deep" (X, 471), and with the "immeasurable Abyss" (VII, 211). Superficially at least, the male-female alterity we have described as the creative exchange between form and matter appears to collapse. Though the "womb / Of unoriginal *Night*" (X, 476-477) parallels the feminine principle of the universe, Chaos can hardly be identified with the masculine principle or order manifested in Christ, the sun, and Adam. What the reader must recognize, it seems to me, is that Night and Chaos are at the farthest extreme from the Light and Order which they may become through divine agency. The symbolic bivalence between Light and Night (which makes the metaphor for male form an exponent of female matter) is explicit when we recall that Milton designates Night "eldest of things" in Book II (962) and identifies "light ethereal" as "first of things, quintessence pure / Sprung from the Deep" in Book VII (243). Light becomes therefore the highest possible refinement of what Night supplies potentially. It is the created agency through which God creates. [8] Chaos, on the other hand, is not so much an inversion of order as it is simply the lack of order. It is the absolute reduction of efficient cause and therefore impotent, though it stands in relation to Night as male to female. Worth repeating is that Milton did not conceive matter as evil or as antithetical to spirit but as the material with which God created the world, itself an attribute of His own nature which may change all to spirit. Chaos and Night, then, exist potentially as male and female in creative union.

---

[8] Professor Watkins is right when he notes that "only in connection with the moon, with her mysterious power over tides and women, is light ever female in Milton" (p. 59). Light is characteristically masculine and the fertilizing agent of all life. Cf. VIII, 95-97; IV, 671-673; V, 300-302; III, 585-586.

Walter Clyde Curry has shown that Milton's doctrine of Chaos and Old Night is in accord with Neoplatonic cosmologies. [9] Proclus, for example, identified Chaos with the second divine principle of the "intelligible triad" and Night with the first procession of the "intelligible and at the same time intellectual triad." Of the three hypostases or emanations of the "intelligible triad," *bound* and *infinity* are analogous to form and matter, though as a whole monad it is masculine and paternal. The "intelligible and at the same time intellectual triad" subsits according to infinity. It is the receptacle of paternal causes, feminine, and maternal. In this way, as Professor Curry says, "Proclus provides for a union of masculine and feminine principles through which original essences are nurtured and transmitted into all posterior being." [10] It is true that the female principle subsists in the primarily masculine order of emanation, but Proclus ascribed this to God's dual nature, signifying thereby the generative or creative power of the One. If Proclus is a valid source for Milton's thought (and Professor Curry believes he is), then Milton had authority for presenting Chaos as a male god in its feminine attribute as "the infinite" or Many-in-One, while at the same time establishing Night, the nurse and receptacle of generation, as the goddess and consort of Chaos. The principle of each in all and all in each explains both Milton's and Proclus' symbolism for representing male and female as subsisting in all orders of emanation from the most nearly perfect down to matter itself. Thus, "male and female principles are found everywhere operative even to the last manifestation of divine power." [11]

Because "shape" or being is an infused principle, matter requires form as the female demands the male:

> Matter unform'd and void: Darkness profound
> Cover'd th' Abyss: but on the wat'ry calm
> His brooding wings the Spirit of God outspread. (VII, 233-235)

As the male principle that gives form, Christ is both the Word and the Spirit (VII, 208-209) and

[9] *Milton's Ontology, Cosmogony, and Physics* (Lexington, Kentucky, 1957), pp. 48-73.
[10] *Ibid.*, p. 53.
[11] *Ibid.*, p. 63.

SEXUAL METAPHOR IN MILTON

... from the first
Wast present, and with mighty wings outspread
Dove-like satst brooding on the vast Abyss
And mad'st it pregnant. (I, 19-22)

In this context, Milton makes the dove, a traditional image of the Holy
Spirit, the unifying symbol of God in His creating powers. One account
held, in fact, that the Virgin Mary conceived when the Holy Ghost
descended in the figure of a dove and whispered in her ear. John
Swan's *Speculum Mundi* (1635), moreover, identified the dove as one
of the animals whose life was a perfect pattern of "chaste, mutual, and
matrimoniall love." [12] Iconographically, the dove also symbolized the
rapture inspired by Venus Urania, the highest exponent of God's
creative powers. In Achille Bocchi's *Symbolicae quaestiones* (1574), for
example, one of the images (defined as *divinus amator*) shows a youthful Mercury contemplating a dove descending on beams of celestial
light. [13] As an image of love, Milton's dove is altogether appropriate
as a symbol of what is truly creative, of a divine *spiritus* empowered
to join "like things to like" (VII, 240), to shape a birth from "Nature's
Womb" (V, 181), to command the Earth to put forth her seed (VII,
309-312), and to make the unreal real (X, 471).

If Milton develops his cosmology from a male-female principle
raised to the highest level of abstraction, one also wonders to what
extent his ontology —or perhaps more exactly, his Christology— corresponds with the physics of nature as we have seen it operate at both
the human and cosmic levels. There is no compelling reason to agree
with Professor Cope when he says that Milton rejected "the physi-
cally elaborated conception of Christ as the spouse of the love-thirsting
soul ...," a tradition Milton would have confronted in the writings of
St. Teresa, St. Bernard, Joseph Beaumont, Donne, and Herbert. [14]
It is true that there is no explicit treatment of such a relationship in
Paradise Lost, but one thinks of Lycidas, who hears "the unexpressive
nuptial Song, / In the blest Kingdoms meek of joy and love," and

[12] Quoted in Kester Svendsen, *Milton and Science* (Cambridge, 1956), p. 163.
[13] See Edgar Wind, *Pagan Mysteries in the Renaissance* (London, 1958),
fig. 20, and his comment p. 108.
[14] Jackson I. Cope, *The Metaphoric Structure of "Paradise Lost"* (Baltimore,
1962), p. 80.

wonders if the weight of tradition can be so easily dismissed. One explains, I think, the willingness of matter to receive the efficient cause of divine potency by seeing its analogy with the willingness of woman to receive man and of mankind to receive God. Both are patterns of the soul's longing for Christ and the manifest desire of "uncreated night" —whatever its level of symbolization— to have form and therefore existence.

More directly relevant to Milton's Christology is the symbolic dominance of the womb as the nexus between God and man. The image gains immeasurably when one remembers that it is the controlling figure of potentiality in matter and that through a symbolic inversion (in the allegorical figure of Sin) it becomes the image of oblivion and extinguished life. Symbolically ambivalent, the womb may either reconcile or disjoin. Impregnated by the "Power of the most High" (XII, 369), the human womb shall yield the Perfect Man, a second Adam; and Eve salutes the Virgin Mother:

> ... Hail,
> High in the love of Heav'n, yet from my Loins
> Thou shalt proceed, and from thy Womb the Son
> Of God most High; so God with man unites. (XII, 379-382)

Thus, the atonement for mankind is the paradigm of mutual love between man and woman, the at-onement of all nature lost with the "sin original." The womb, therefore, mediates separation and relieves the unbearable disjunction of sexual opposites as well as the spiritual sterility of man without God. [15]

It was inevitable that Neoplatonic theologists should see in the trinitarian concept of the Christian Godhead a parallel to the triadic formulas of Proclus and the hypostases of Plotinus. Both Ficino and

---

[15] It is interesting that one of Adam's responses to the growing understanding of his fallen condition is a desire to "be Earth / Insensible" (X, 776-777), and more: "how glad would lay me down / As in my Mother's lap" (X, 777-778). The psychology here is that Adam wants to return to uncreated innocence, in modern terms, to return to the womb where love is unconditional and requires no responsibilities. Adam has failed to earn his father's love (i. e., God's), which was conditional in its demanded obedience ("wilt thou enjoy the good, / Then cavil the conditions? ..." [X, 758-759]). In consequence of his failure, Adam desires to escape from all knowledge of his act of separation and, like Satan, to lose himself in "the womb / Of unoriginal *Night* and *Chaos* wild" (X, 477).

Pico, however, denied that Plotinus' second hypostasis —the Intelligence— could be equated with the second person of the Trinity; yet neither was deterred from tracing St. Augustine's *vestigia trinitatis* through all the levels of the Neoplatonic system. [16] If the persons of the Trinity could be seen as analogous to the progressions of Neoplatonic emanation, then it was also possible to conceive the Trinity in terms of triadic sexuality. However much the logic of such identification was wrenched, the Neoplatonists could always find authority in Dionysius' *De divinis nominibus,* where the rule was that "incongruous symbols are the best." [17] In one passage of *Paradise Lost* there appears to be a survival of these Neoplatonic ideas. Milton's lines express the relationship between God and Christ in terms strikingly parallel to those he uses to describe Eve's relationship to Adam:

> He [God] said, and on his Son with Rays direct
> Shone full; hee all his Father full exprest
> Ineffably into his face receiv'd. (VI, 719-721)

Like the Earth and the Moon receiving the rays of the Sun, Christ is exalted by the effulgence of God. Christ's symbolic attribute is feminine, while God's is masculine. Like Eve's praise of Adam, Christ declares of God:

> ... thou always seek'st
> To glorify thy Son, I always thee,
> As is most just; this I my glory account,
> My exaltation, and my whole delight,
> That thou in me well pleas'd, declar'st thy will
> Fulfill'd, which to fulfil is all my bliss. (VI, 724-729)

"I in thee / For ever," Christ continues, and recognizes himself as the image of God in all things (VI, 732-736).

Spenser's treatment of the "faire loue" of God for Sapience in "An Hymne of Heavenly Beavtie" is illustrative of the symbolic technique Milton employs to translate Christ into the feminine attributes of Godhead. The love relationship Spenser describes between God and Sapience, the goddess Wisdom of Hebrew scripture, fuses Greek

[16]. *De Trinitate,* VIII, x, 14. Cf. Wind, p. 44.
[17] Cited in Wind, p. 49, n. 1.

and Hebraic traditions something after the fashion of St. Paul. [18] Following one of the prevailing traditions in the Renaissance, Spenser conventionally identifies her with Christ, thus linking them symbolically and reflecting the popular Renaissance idea of a male and female relationship between the first and second persons of the Trinity. His description of Sapience also suggests the female figure of the Song of Songs:

> There in his bosome *Sapience* doth sit,
> The soueraine dearling of the *Deity*, ...
>
> Let Angels which her goodly face behold
> And see at will, her soueraigne praises sing,
> And those most sacred mysteries vnfold,
> Of that faire loue of mightie heauens king ...
>
> And lets his owne Beloued to behold. [19]

Thus, Sapience is the queen of Heaven and iconographically represents one attribute of Christ.

Now, it would be patently absurd to press this point much further: Milton's dominant conception of the Son is as the figure *Christus victor*; in relation to man, He is a second Adam, the image of Reason triumphant. But the lines cited here do manifest a conception of Christ that subordinates Him to God in the same way that Eve is subordinated to Adam in prelapsarian Eden. God and Christ subsist therefore as two attributes (to some extent analogous to male and female) within a triadic formula completed by the Holy Ghost, which together acts as the efficient cause of generation.

Thus, the externalization into the cosmos of sex symbols derived chiefly from human experience is Milton's celebration of the divine creative process. It is Milton's hymn to the *act* of creation and his assertion that as God creates with His sudden Word, so man creates with the generative power, physical and spiritual, with which he is

---

[18] See 1 Corinthians 1. 24: "But unto them which are called, both Jews and Greeks, Christ the power of God, and the wisdom of God."

[19] In *The Works of Edmund Spenser: The Minor Poems,* ed. Charles G. Osgood and Henry Gibbons Lotspeich (Baltimore, 1943), I, 227-229.

invested. If it is true, as C. S. Lewis maintained, [20] that Milton believed in a higher value than human love, it is also true that that value is an extension of what we know through the agency of human love. For Milton, love is the source of all being, an expression of what is Real: without it, we are cut off from what is truly creative; we lie "a great Prince in prison"; and instead of life we embrace death and lust and hate, and we work our own destruction.

Tulane University   PURVIS E. BOYETTE

---

[20] *Preface to "Paradise Lost"* (London, 1942), p. 127.